A Course in Light

A Spiritual Path for Enlightenment

Channeled by

Antoinette Moltzan

Series 4

Planetary 7- 9

A Course in Light

Written and Channeled by
Antoinette Moltzan
Copyright 1973 by Antoinette Moltzan
Revised 2003

Published by Az Reality Publishers

Printed in United State of America

Library of Congress

Cataloging in Publication Data

Certificate of Registration

04/26/2001

ISBN 0-9710490-5-X

Dedication

I would like to dedicate A Course in Light to all the people who have made this series of meditation lessons so exciting and joyful. To all the students and those who are just discovering this path of light I dedicate this work to each of you.

Recognition

I would like to give thanks and appreciation to Karen Yahraus, Kristin Lindquist for editing this Series 4 of *A Course in Light*. I wish to give thanks to Vicki Yang for her dedication to the translation of this course for the Chinese version. I wish to recognize all the teachers here in the states and abroad for dedicating time and their lives to the teaching of this path of light.

I especially give thanks and honor to the unseen teachers of the light who have transmitted this work through the process of channeling.

Table of Contents

Section One

Table of Contents

Section Two

Table of Contents

Section Three

SECTION ONE

PLANETARY 7

HEALING PYRAMIDS

LESSONS OF THE MIND

&

KEYS & CODES OF CONSCIOUSNESS

INTRODUCTION

The light meditations continue as given to us by the masters of the White Brotherhood. As you move through Planetary 7, you increase the energy field around you and work with a pyramid structure of five sides. The increase in the energy field affects you in many unique ways. Only you can determine how it manifests.

This level brings you through the inner planes to expand your personal energy system. You receive the *Lessons of Mind* as you move into the Planetary Center and the networking of light.

You go deep into the silence entering the Pyramid of Light and bring into the pyramid those who are in need of healing and change in conditions. Always ask permission from the higher self and soul body of anyone you wish to bring into the Pyramid of Light. If you feel, see or experience good energy, you know it is right to bring them into the light. If you sense resistance, heaviness or darkness, accept this as a sign that you are not to interfere with their lessons.

The true ingredients to healing are **acceptance**, **release** and **forgiveness**. As you release judgments about a situation, you release your perspective on how a situation should be. This clears your own personal thoughts in order to connect to the Higher Power or your inner guidance.

The Will of the Father/Creator is not always the will of the personality, which sees things from its limited perspective. However, by bringing the *little will* into alignment with the *Higher Will* you release the power of the light for its greater effect. Through the process of meditation, willfulness is tested. The goal is to align with your *Higher Will.*

As groups study these messages and connect with the light work, coming together each week strengthens the bond and sharing. It also increases the light energy and you will feel its awesome power. As you come together in circles to focus on healing and love, your openness for support adds to your own healing. When you hold each other in the light, seeing love as the absolute source, the connection from the light energy magnifies the healing. The power of the work of light brings change. The group work is very important in maintaining and clearing any form of negative consciousness.

In your group circle, visualizations for release can be an absolute positive experience. As an example, if the emotional self is filled with anger, past regret, sorrow and is weighing heavy in someone's experience, have each one focus on the student's emotional body.

Perceive you are creating a large body of energy in the color of the week, perhaps in the form of a hot air balloon. Focus on this balloon as a body of energy and see yourself rising up into it. Visualize all negativity being released into this sphere of energy.

Feel yourself lifted as you let go of holding onto the physical senses. As you feel the movement of the energy and release the negativity, slowly direct the balloon to the higher levels.

Then imagine you are letting go of all the negative attachments to your body, mind and spirit. You will feel the negativity being released.

This visualization procedure can magnify the release of any discontents and is applicable to any of the light rays.

As you descend into the physical plane, accept that you are cleared and freed from discontent.

The **meditation procedure** for Planetary 7 is similar to the previous planetary lessons. For more in-depth understanding, you may wish to study the book, *The Book of Knowledge, The Keys of Enoch.*[1] This is an in-depth, scientific account of what transpires through the continuing and progressive evolution of all light forms. The book is a channeled writing under the Order of Enoch. With the keys of this book, you begin to integrate more thoroughly the understanding of the pyramids of light and their connection to the inner planes.

Your courage to move into these higher dimensions is recognized by the masters as well as your own spirit and soul. What you gain, you pass on to others. Let light and love shine on your way through the extended journey of self-growth.

---

[1] The book of Knowledge, Keys of Enoch J. J. Hurtak

MEDITATION PROCEDURE

Become still.

Gather your awareness into the center of the forebrain. Call forth all egos, bringing them into one unified consciousness.

Consciously direct these unified egos up through the lower dimensions into the soul body and into the center of the White Light.

Expand the White Light and create a whirlpool to clear and close off your energy field.

Move back into the center of the White Light and activate all the centers of your soul body of light.

Expand your energy field to encompass each of your fellow soul mates in your group, forming one unified group vibration.

As a unified group vibration, move up through the central vertical axis through the White Light and into the center of the Silver Chalice, activating and expanding this light.

Move up through the Rainbow Bridge into your own planetary center. Move into the temple and merge with the master of your destiny, your guides, your teachers and all of the hierarchy.

Within this gathering of souls, feel and experience the merging of your vibration with all students of your group, as well as all light workers throughout the planet.

Merge with the Council of Light and all beings flowing on this frequency of light (color of the week) from the higher realms. Take a few moments to attune your vibration to this frequency at the planetary level.

Move into the network of light surrounding the planet earth, directing the light into the aura and throughout the bodies of the planet. Flow with your guidance into those areas in need of healing.

Move back into your own planetary center and into the temple, the inner chamber of your Higher Mind.

As you move into the silence to commune with your own spirit, ask for the knowledge needed for your own individual growth.

As you return from the silence, begin your descent through Mind to the Rainbow Bridge and into your lower nature. Feel the frequencies of light within your planetary center flow through the Rainbow Bridge into the centers of your soul body

Create your own healing pyramid from the center of the White Light expanding outward and surrounding your being. Expand this pyramid to 150 feet and call forth all those who are in need of healing and upliftment.

When you have completed your healing work, ground your energies into the Black Power Center.

Lesson One

COLOR RAY: WHITE

The Light of Purification

Activate the meditation procedure

Message & Meditation #1

I speak with wisdom to you who listen and hear. I greet your joyous spirits of light. I come with an open mind to hear you. Joy connects to the source of your own spirit. You come again to experience the vibrations that bring connection to the Higher Self. The Lightwork given to this point is a process of opening up resources within you to experience a new phase of evolving consciousness. In this session the lesson is what *the evolving self truly means*. Evolving means moving from one step to another, regardless of the conditions or effects that brought one into a place of challenge. To evolve means to move through the challenge into a phase where you recreate from a higher perspective. Regardless of errors created, they all can be reassessed and changes in consciousness affect the way your experiences unfold.

Evolving through choice means to let go of the instinctive concept you must function as a survival vibration or in a behavioral pattern instigated by fear. You may fear you will lose your dreams, hopes and wishes. Whatever fear remains in you, this element can control the results in your life.

You must make the move from survival to evolution. This is transpiring in the present time. You are evolving as you allow yourself to experience activity from a perspective of **trust, will** and **free-flowing** from within to without.

Each one in the inner planes receives the teachings of the council. You become very aware you are connected as your body senses and registers the frequency of light through the resources of your own soul consciousness. At times, the conscious mind may not fully comprehend or perceive what is transpiring. You know through faith, there are realities within these inner levels you seek to incorporate.

Let go of the fear your choices will undermine you and your life experiences, as this is the greatest barrier to your sense of inner peace.

Wisdom comes through discovery; discovery comes from the movement through the undetected or unknown. You constantly live by the source of knowing the unknown. You must walk without a sense of direction from any source, other than received by your own intuitive senses. This is how wisdom becomes integrated.

The masters come incarnate through this particular experience and gifts of the spirit are becoming more prevalent to those who ask. When you seek only the counsel of others, you are closing off the counsel of your own intuitive senses. Yes, you have challenges of the body and the material plane that seem to cause barriers to your receiving personal instruction, but you must walk step-by-step totally with a degree of wisdom and faith. As faith is active and belief is accepted, then connection to the source is already fully experienced. It is the anxiety and the doubt; it is the sense of being in resistance to your source of good that closes the door to your receiving.

Lighted Ones have come to the earth through many millenniums of time, reconstructing the patterns and dramas of their former existences into present-time activity. As entities and initiates of this particular pathway of light, you also have your dramas unfolding in and about you. The dramas contain many persons you have lived with and known. Often their particular lives create resistances within the will of your own being. You find that you are pulling at opposite poles, creating resistances and anger setting off a barrier to experiencing the intuitiveness of your lighted self.

As you meditate, find yourself letting go of fear you are in loss, and blocked from The Source. Affirm in a positive projected manner, your oneness with God, Light and all that you are as a being of light.

Planetary Light Work

As workers within this plane of expression, you have consented to direct the light through the network of energy to ease the heaviness within the earth system. Again, we perceive containment of the crises of nuclear forecasts. The reality of nuclear explosiveness creates nothing but darkness and void, a deadness of all things upon the planet. This is impressed upon the minds of the leaders of many nations. With this in full view and understanding, there is a lessening of this as a personal threat to any country. Therefore, the highest peak of nuclear encounter has dissipated. But again, as long as the weaponry exists, as long as the experience can be activated under an impulse, there is always the fear that it will mount and come into being.

Therefore, the continuous vibration of light directed towards those who defend and work in these vibrations of militant consciousness is required. Direct the rays of light into mental processes and re-affirm that these factions begin to lay down the arms, releasing the need to war against themselves.   Perceive the peace and preparation of the Christ Spirit overseeing the evolving action of human consciousness.   Perceive the energies directed into pyramidal structures. This is your particular vehicle of light that overshadows all of your physical senses. This is the temple of your spirit formulated into geometrical design, for it is the most perfect energy transformer that exists in universal consciousness. The pyramids reflect the perfect geometrical angles in which energy is the most powerful.

As you are flowing within the radiant frequency of the White Light, be in touch with the gifts of your higher self. The gift of wisdom is an attunement to truth that already lies within the source of who you are. Your wisdom unfolds through its practical activity, but the discernment between what is important on a practical level and what seems to be the resources of wisdom, is a battle. You will find through this cycle a speeding up of your processes. Wisdom becomes a true point of your experience. How you receive wisdom, comes from meeting the challenges of the unknown.

Perceive you are within the radiant purified energy of the White Light. See the pyramid in its five-sided vibration, all in the purity of the White Light. Center within this particular essence and let the body absorb vibrations of this energy. Any issues that have been unresolved, ask that there be purity and clearing of pure understanding, clearness of vision.   The essence of energy envelops you as you call forth all those who have been a part of your experience.

As you can see, you are really a part of many. You are participating in visions of light in which you are seeing changes in the energy structures of consciousness. Many of the pictures you have connected with are projections for change in the earth and the process of its own clearing. If a waterfall you see suddenly becomes dry, you are experiencing a shift in the earth's particular flow. When you see waters running in places that had been a desert, you are also seeing a change in consciousness within and without. As you observe different movements within yourself, you are experiencing energy connecting to areas within your own spirit, soul and physical reality preparing for its own vibrational change.

The earth is in a new vibration. It is in a new frequency rate. How does this occur? Through a gathering of many and the focus on a shift in vibrational rhythms within thought, emotion and physical realities, a wave of change occurs within human mind, human thought and human expression. These waves of change have brought sudden and abrupt new realities into human life. You are experiencing a shift in the total experience of living on the planet. It is a time of great celebration and extraordinary awareness of challenges yet to be met. Celebrations of change are truly an inward consciousness and often an outward demonstration. Hassles with all the change for free choice in life is the power of resistance to deny life freedom. You are seeing the battles in effect.

Beloved students accept and know your experiences through mind, thought, soul and through spirit as light, have created a link to this change. You participate in the movement. You participate in the event. Your consciousness is opening up each moment you are expressing the light.

As your physical self perceives its struggle to come to realizations, it is changing what and who you are associating with and the light brings the change for others. The bond, the correspondence is a connection fulfilling a spiritual law.

In this moment, think in terms:

The more I clear my own essence, the more my essence becomes a clearing vehicle for all who walk as a part of it.

When you complete your meditation or group experience, focus on returning to your body and ground your energy in and through the Black Power Ray.

Keys & Codes of Consciousness

The Keys & Codes of Consciousness is an encoded meditative procedure using symbols and affirmations. Each symbol is a coded vibratory pattern known as the language of Light. Each key is an affirmation, which magnifies the energy of Light.

Work with each code and key for one week at a time. Visualize the symbol in your daily life. As you practice meditating with the symbol and keys, you may experience your own patterns or codes given to you. Write in a personal journal your insights, experiences and revelations as they come to you. In keeping a record of your experiences, observe your growth and personal expansion in consciousness.

The Council of Light presented the messages that accompany these keys and codes. Each session brings similar messages and experiences.

Key & Code 1

THE EYE

The Code is The Eye

The Codes & Keys are the language of the soul and spirit. They are the direct communication byways you use to connect with other forms of life.

The Eye in the capstone of the pyramid represents, I AM THAT I AM, the all knowing, all seeing, eye of soul consciousness.

The Key is the mantra:

I AM THAT I AM.
I AM IN MY KNOWING AND MY SEEING.
I SEE WHAT I KNOW.
I KNOW WHAT I SEE.
I ACCEPT WITHOUT QUESTION.

The path each of you chose to walk is a path of messengers, healers and transformers of conscious ego systems. You seek to attain reality as co-creators of Spirit and Mind in Light. The keys and codes presented in this course create in thought; direct impulses upon the soul plane and transmit into soul creative energy.

Each key is a symbol bringing to the soul a conceptual idea relating to an image that stimulates an energy process for manifestation. Azreal presented the formula in thought as mind-manna, light energy and manifestation.

The keys are the language of the soul and spirit. They are the direct communication byways you use to connect with other forms of life.

Mind is the first coded key you will receive in this experience. The Mind is the symbol known as the Eye. The Eye is the all-seeing, the all-knowing, I AM.

The Eye, centered in the capstone of the pyramid relates to the consciousness of the Higher Mind and corresponds to your own center of the Higher Self. This is the energy pattern and code recognized as the essence that sees and knows, observes creativity and consciousness in motion.

The Eye relates to your inner eye connected to the glands in the body known as the pineal and pituitary.

Ask what you are willing to see, what you must know in order to see. Ask insight to be clear. In your meditation practice becoming one with I AM.

Now speak inwardly:

I AM THAT I AM.
I AM IN MY KNOWING AND MY SEEING.
I SEE WHAT I KNOW.
I KNOW WHAT I SEE.
I ACCEPT WITHOUT QUESTION.

Message

Each key creates in you a new direction and the key in effect, Key 1, as spoken by the hierarchy, opens you to see more of everything that truly is. From the *ancient schools of mystery* this is known, as the center of the eye representing the Eye of the *I Am of All That Is*. The Eye is the link through all your many lives assisting you to understand and see your past.

As spoken by our brothers of the council, you are all initiates from the ancient days, the beginning of the earth's first experience of human life. You have come from many journeys of life, having attained and maintained a status of sacred consciousness. You are remembering as we speak your first initiations to and within the Order of Melchizedek.

The first key, the Eye often seen in the center of the pyramid represents trust in the One God, trust in the oneness of all that is and awareness of seeing past illusions of human consciousness.

As we speak, focus on the Eye within you. In meditation, many see eyes looking at them. Perceive yourself looking through a consciousness taking you into inner planes of awareness. So as it is, think and be:

I see what I know; I know what I see;
I accept unconditionally.

When this becomes your mantra, all surrounding you clears the way to see all that is meant to be. This key activates a deeper level of your insight. It opens the channel in you to have understanding beyond what you know in conscious thinking. There are many mysteries connected to this eye. Each of you will find its deeper meaning when you meditate within this process.

There are many ways to see. Seeing is not looking outwardly but experiencing your knowing inwardly. The Eye is a sacred step in progress, not a tool but a state of consciousness.

The key and coding is activated into everything a part of you. So once again the mantra is,

I see what I know; I know what I see;
I accept unconditionally.

When this becomes a state of being, your level of inner peace is unquestionable and the power of the Eye is recognized as the source that breaks through illusions around you. One more time,

I see what I know, I know what I see and I
accept it unconditionally.

By the Order of Melchizedek, the essence comes through to encode you with this insight.

Tests may present themselves in accordance to your individual consciousness. Illusions may appear so strong that the sight is dark and the fear becomes your challenge. Remember this mantra, and watch all resistances release. Priests, priestesses, ministers, messengers, perceivers, wisdom givers, light bearers, shamans of medicines are all one, each of you with degrees of personal unfoldment.

The pyramids of Egypt represent centers and vortexes of the earth. They are energy points of the planet and have always been a source of mystery to the human curiosity. Though perceived to be the tombs of great kings and leaders of past time, they also hold the keys and codes of mystery that are reflective of the Golden Age. Though the sands of time have washed away some of the outer factors of these symbols, the secret chambers still exists, the hall of records still are untapped, it shall be opened.

So now, think of yourself in the total center of the Eye and ask that the records of your soul reveal enough for you to follow through with the commission you came here to do.

The pressure you feel around the head and forebrain is the energy flow seeking to break the veils placed around you. They will not be broken before it is time; it is all in the hands of your acceptance. So now, beloved one, observe how you become a part of this breakthrough for your sight.

Let the Eye of the center of this key and code activate in you, transforming to new awakenings within you.

When you are ready to anchor what is given, find yourself coming back into the consciousness of the physical world surrounding you. As you begin to flow back to the physical body and into the senses of your physical self, feel the power of Light coming through and anchoring you. Know you are in a total state of oneness.

Go in peace and may the Light of the Christ be in and through you.

Lesson Two

COLOR RAY: GOLD

The Light of Transmutation –The Cosmic Father

Activate the Meditation Procedure

Message & Meditation #1

I greet you in the name of the Father and of the Spirit of Christ, which is indwelling within your consciousness. It is with great pleasure we greet you once again and merge with your being to uplift any discordant activity within the physical selves.

Rise up through the frequency centers, through the rays of energy, and into the higher planetary center, in which your vibration exists as pure light, pure mind and radiant sound. The influx of planetary energies through the cycles of planetary work is most needed energies for those who gather in circles of light to direct the rays into the earth system.

You are overseers of the evolution of the total human system and this is the highest desire that one's soul can express. We bring this understanding into your consciousness at this time, for you are in an intense cycle of initiation which is preparing you to meet those conditions and desires which have brought your soul into incarnation within the earth plane many times.

If growth could transpire without the needed lessons, there would be no life within the earth. Judge not yourself harshly, nor perceive self unworthy. Man's judgments are based upon false-to-fact concepts, which blind him to the true clear vision.

Know that all who have accepted their pathway of discipleship have experienced periods of time when there was the inner void, when there was the *dark night of the soul*, when there is a sense of losing self to materiality and that reality. During these times, all have experienced anxiety and despair. As the awakening to the inner cause is remembered, there is the release; wisdom comes through the experience of release. Therefore, your material level is seen as a place in which you live, move and have your being. Focus on bringing the vibration of healing into this reality.

Again, the full focus of your purpose is to be an emissary of the consciousness of the discipleship of The Christ. Christ means the *over self of the spirit* which brings reality of truth into a conscious direction. You are becoming an emissary of this direct message. You are the bearers of spirit and truth who pour forth their consciousness to those who are open to receive. When the minds of those around you are open, you begin to feel the intensity of the flow of consciousness and you become the instrument through which the healing process transpires. First uplift yourself.

As the essence of light in the frequency of the Golden Ray is moving in and throughout your vibration, perceive alignment. You will find yourself receiving in accordance with your openness. Perceive your outer life unfolding with a greater sense of inner joy and contentment.

When all of the wills align, there is a knowingness you are flowing with a constant activity directed by the will of the soul. You experience a moving of your total life with a greater ease. This is not to say you will live without the challenges and difficulties of lessons, but there flows within you an understanding you are moving in accordance with a design imprinted upon your soul consciousness. Perceive that the perfection of your life emanates through the choices and challenges brought before you.

Now perceive this frequency of the Golden Ray transmuting all thought patterns and mental imageries holding you bound to the concepts of negative past activity. Release all anxiety about earthly conditions that appear to be inharmonious to your soul's nature and desire. Perceive the body moving intensely into new vibrations. Perceive all personal concerns and worries released from the conscious level. Receive the activity of the higher will, the will of the Father fully and completely.

The movement through self-evolution is a very intense acceleration on every level of consciousness. As you perceive the light integrating with the cosmic element of your inner being and incorporate the higher vision within all systems of thought, you see the greater good with increasing clarity and project the essence of higher expression outwardly.

The Masters sees all as spirit and light. You may strive to understand the conscious self and work within that realm to help uplift any activity in conflict. The inner self, however, is the true part of you that recognizes a divine essence.

Look beyond the egos and see the spirit. You will find the love and unification. To focus on the diversities and the imageries creates the negations. See self mirrored through the consciousness of light and the activity of the highest spirit.

Planetary Light Work

Moving with the network of energy, direct the Radiant Golden energy in and through the triangulations or grids of energy surrounding the earth. Let your spirit and soul travel to instill the light within all areas that are in need of vibration for upliftment and healing.

Yes, beloved ones, your elder brothers in light shall descend to communicate internationally to alleviate the destructive forces moving into escalation. There will be encounters with this vibration. There is much protection in and around all of your consciousness, but also know the warring forces that oppose recognition of individual spirit must be uplifted by The Mind and the light. Perceive yourself as one vibration amongst millions and billions of lighted spirits.

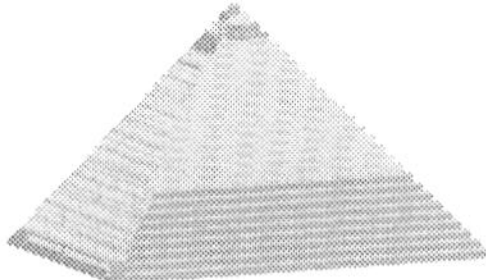

Now move with your awareness down through the Rainbow Bridge of Light. Once again, focus within the soul center as we bring the pyramidal structure into being. At this point, you are familiar with these vehicles of energy and awareness and you form the structures instantaneously through mind. Perceive the Radiant Silver Ray moving into the magnetic side and back, the Radiant White Light upon the dynamic side and the front, with the essence of the Cosmic Father upon the base. Feel yourself enveloped in these frequencies.

If there are those within your thoughts who are in need of healing, call their souls into this center of light and bring them into this vibration, asking that their higher selves accept the energies to transmute dis-ease and negations within their bodies. Do not try to measure the effect; let the cause, which is the light be magnified. Allow yourself to be free from curiosity, letting the energy be the healer.

When you are ready, focus your awareness into the forebrain and draw all of your egos back into this point.

Ground your consciousness.

Give thanks for the joy of sharing yourself and all of your consciousness.

Be at peace.

Message & Meditation #2

Andrew

Truth flows from the heart as well as from the awareness of your spirit, bringing to your heart a sense of its own magnificence. Each of you are presented with opportunities to experience the power of your own true essence. As the channel has presented the image for each of you to reflect upon, you draw from this experience, clarity in thought for change in your present being.

Ask that you become free from illusion and diverse conditions blocking your sense of direction. Ask for understanding. Ask love to have its flow in you without fear. Ask for a sense of being present in each and all moments of your daily living. Ask for release of conditional thoughts that block your power from expressing itself in its most beautiful and natural way. All these aspects presented move into the vibration of light and all the hues of energy in Gold are magnified.

 All Gold

The pyramids of light now activated from your own higher self are a result of your own higher vision and thought. So take a moment in this time to feel the energy in the pyramid structures and recognize these designs as a total prism of light, perfect in its design, perfect in its energy flow, perfect in its correspondency to your pattern and to your particular position within your initiatory experience.

The power of the pyramid never is fully revealed, either to man or to spirit. It is a doorway through the unconscious to inner planes. All pyramids, all the many different designs and colors, affect consciousness for specific purposes of change. The structure most active for this position is the Golden Pyramid in its many-sided design. Bring into it all you are seeking to change, fulfill and become.

As liberation and freedom are the key words for the planet, within yourself you are liberated from karmic causes, limitations of emotion, thought and action.

I Andrew, speak to you.

In this moment, a golden key is, presented. With this key, perceive it as a symbol that unlocks, within all you have been, the fears of imprisonment, of limitation, of enslavement, of persecution, of humiliation, of rejection, of isolation and of death. As the key unlocks the vibrations stored, not yet touched by light, feel the release of these within and experience the explosion of change. Expect the transformation as absolute. When the void has become a result of release, then the in-flowing light can manifest in its place.

The light of this Golden Ray directs conscious thoughts to joyful acceptance of life, success and achieving steps in your path. Your path is your journey of adventure and growth. Each step you have taken in your journey has its footprint impressed within you. Know each step, each footprint has its own message, acknowledge it as an important part of your wholeness. Though many of these impressions and imprints have been harsh, difficult, confusing, unclear and misdirected, each has brought you deeper levels of wisdom, understanding and strength.

In this moment, the council greets all of you and those who follow in these patterns of meditative experiences. The council greets each one with great celebration. As thoughts of liberation and freedom are magnified in you, perceive them connecting to all in the planet earth. As nations rise to the changes in consciousness, to preparations for new ideals of thought in life expression, send with these thoughts, the light to the human family, those who are as you, initiates in consciousness of life.

As you envision freedom becoming a personal opportunity for all human life, know you have played a part in it becoming a reality. The power of your experiences, through these meditative expressions, adds to the consciousness of change.

Let yourself become full-bodied in the light, fully aware in the moment and totally connected with all that ancient spirits have presented. Know that the past is now, and all the tomorrows are now. You create the vision. Send the thought again that the earth turning towards the light is protected against the powers of resistance.

Now each and all of you are more effective in your direction and your thought. The acceleration of you, your pathways, lessons and your soul's commitment to growth are truly an absolute. Let go of your worries, concerns, denials and fears and let the hands of light heal. Let the minds of light transform. Go in peace.

Key & Code 2

The Flame

The Code is The Flame

This is the energy representing the purification transpiring through direct connection with matter to Light. Matter put into the flame of Light transforms.

Meditate on the Flame and the thought of accepting guidance through the passageway to the point of Light. Meditate on acceptance of your Mind to the energies before you and between you and the God/Creator, Father/Mother of All.

The Key is the mantra:

I AM AS MIND.
I AM AS MANNA.
I AM AS LIGHT.
I AM MANIFESTING.
LET THERE BE LIGHT IN ALL.

Message #1

Andrew

It is good to speak to those who come receiving the keys to the codes of spirit. We introduced into this pathway the first key known as the Eye.

Now we present the coded key recognized as The Flame.

When you look at candlelight, you see a flame. This is energy representing purification transpiring through direct connection with matter to Light. Matter put to the Flame of Light is changed. The Flame is also perceived through the historical patterns of teachings *as the tongue of God*, meaning the fire and light of the spoken word. Focus on the Flame. It's colors become golden in hues and changes from red and gold to white.

Each of these represents certain parts of the work of energy in process of transforming denseness into Manna or Mind. Therefore, the chakra center of your soul is the gold hues of light. The crown of kings and queens represent the position of dominance over their subjects. The flame relates to the Golden Crown Chakra. It is a code to change what lower mind (manna) has created in opposition to the spiritual self.

The Key is:

I AM AS MIND.
I AM AS MANNA.
I AM AS LIGHT.
I AM MANIFESTING.
LET THERE BE LIGHT IN ALL.

You are in the Flame. The Flame, the torch of Light, passes on from one to another representing the eternality of consciousness. The Flame lights the way to the dark corners of your path. It lights the hallways through the tunnel of your initiation. It consumes the darkness and lightens the way. Without the Flame, there is no fire. Without the fire, there is no desire. Without desire, there is no need and without need, there is no consciousness to become.

Some mental thoughts about the symbol of the flame often are fear. The Flame is, also perceived as an action of evil, or as the *deceivers tool*.   In truth, it is the symbol of transformation or transmutation. For without the Light or the flame, you cannot see your way.   The fire or flame can destroy what is no longer purposeful in consciousness. The key of The Flame is a conscious tool consuming through Mind what needs change.

I AM AS MIND.
I AM AS MANNA.
I AM AS LIGHT.
I AM MANIFESTING.
LET THERE BE LIGHT IN ALL.

Through each experience of this Code and Key, purification takes place within the cells and matter of life. As you experience this flame of Light moving and in through you, observe how it guides you through the passageway preparing you for the next key of Light.

All through history of humanity, fire is perceived as a basic need of survival. It has much consciousness connected with the mystery of life. You discover its deeper meaning for you.

Meditations for this particular period will be on the Code and Key of the Flame. Accept the guidance through the passageway to the point of Light. Accept your mind, the energies before you, between you and the God/Creator, Father/Mother of All enveloped in The Flame.

Message #2

This is Azreal

I speak to you to help assist you in this moment. Do not be concerned, all is in its perfect order and the teachings coming through are right for you. Christ Consciousness blesses it all. The Creator Aspect of you is in the will of the destiny of your spirit. The will of the destiny of your spirit is connected to the records of your soul, manifesting through what your choices are for you. We see the work of Light in the destined path of what you have chosen to explore and to present it to the many who can heal their consciousness.

So though you seem so few in this phase of the work of Light, the power impacted with this work will reach those in need. You will see how miracles unfold. The Keys and Codes are manifesting as symbols of your past. They assist and empower you. The energy of the Lightwork is part of all things within your soul's activity.

Now, as council stands in this sacred moment, each of you are very important and all of you have known each other before. Each have struggled through so many obstacles in this life yet they are much less than lives before and there is much more freedom to achieve what you desire to create right now.

The light of love comes through and surrounds you. Go in peace and may the Light of the Christ be in and through you.

Lesson Three

COLOR RAY: BLUE

The Light of Wisdom

Activate the Meditation Procedure

Message & Meditation #1

Greetings, this is Azreal. I speak again to you as individuals, as well as to all who will read these words. You are the overseers and directors of new thought coming from the ancient wisdom given to humanity through all ages of time. You hold the key in the seeds of the soul. The key within the soul is the key of light and love, that aspect which connects you to the One Source, blending with all energies of the universe. *Think on these things.*

Wisdom will never be, fully understood by the reasoning mind or intellect, regardless of its evolved consciousness. Wisdom is not knowledge, but wisdom holds patterns of energy connecting to The Creative Source which functions in an absolute, unwavering and constant state of energy.

Each vibration you understand in frequency of light is connected to certain laws that oversee creation.   The Lord of Wisdom is a name in the ancient written scripts of The Holy Bible.

Each name represented as God within the scriptures, apply to aspects of God. God is the total consciousness of all creation, exemplified in myriad aspects by thought, word, action, deed and the creative process.   God is not limited to an image as one identity, but is a composite of all identities and egos that function as certain Lords of Life.

The disciples of the Christ which are many, but exemplified by twelve under the teachings of Jesus, are not lords of creations, not lords of karma, are not identities of certain frequency bands, nor are they of the angelic seraphim and cherubim. They are souls, as you, who came into the earth at a particular point in time to carry forth the knowledge and the teachings of the Higher Lords of planetary vibration. Jesus, the Christ, is the Lord of Light showed the way to the soul's pathway into immortality. He, as the Christ, is the way in which the soul connects to its on-going, evolving self. Within the life of Jesus, He exemplified Himself in healing and in Divine Love. He will not be identified by any one message. His message always has a lesson of vital force and never becomes dull. It is always an instigator, up lifter and healer of negative activity. *Think on these things* so you may understand a greater reality within yourself.

You are connecting to these vibrations that ride through the ethers to bring light and healing into all the forces of the earth plane.

Visualize, in this moment, the earth itself spewing off the fears and conflicts. See the lessons of the earth not bound by the karmic repetitions of fear and death, but sense the consciousness of cosmic realities become unfolded in all of the human self and rise like the light. The earth will know its time of peace when the human species gives up its pain, fear and death by self-inflicted experiences, and wears with itself the light of wisdom and peace.

This message has rung true through all generations, but has never received the impact as in this particular time. We see many groups coming out of the cave of their own ignorance into the Mind of Light, intellect, reasoning and re-aligning self towards a cosmic reality.

We do understand as you walk away from meditation and step back into the physical earth, you encounter obstacles you cannot always rise above. Also know these crises and challenges are an indication of the karma of humanity, unclear about its nature and clinging to the patterns of repetitious destruction. In recognizing these patterns, reinstate your affirmation to become an emissary of truth.

This dissertation is for your conscious selves to absorb the frequency of wisdom, feel it implanted within your being. Do not fear yourself failing these words and actions, but recognize the seeds of these higher thoughts are within you and about you.

 Silver, Gold & Blue

"What is the essence and purpose for the pyramids and the magnetic fields created by thought under a discipline of structure? Why are we under these particular pyramidal systems?" and, "What is the total connection to the meditation and the work of light?"

Each pyramid structure is a vibratory creative, geometrical design, which corresponds to a certain plane of soul evolution. In this particular pyramid structure in the Wisdom Ray, with the Magnetic Silver, the Radiant Gold as dynamic and the essence of White, you are blending within yourself the energy to create and transmute negative patterns of your past karmic experience. You open your vibration to a higher evolved experience. Each initiatory plateau is associated with Lessons of Mind and frequencies of light. This is clear in your awakening at the point where soul no longer attaches to the body. You will reinstate and re-live what you are now consciously put into motion. You have cleared much from your soul's vibration allowing you to move quickly through the total process.

Now perceive as egos have descended through the inner vertical axis, the light and frequency bands of energy. You center within this structure of light. All that are a part of you come into this inner vibrational space. Simply see them being uplifted and healing individually and as a family group. Release each one to their own experience, to their own sacred journey through light, love, growth, experience, challenge, lessons and activity. Judge not their path. Go with new strength, wisdom and light.

Message & Meditation #2

Joshua

There is a great tribulation and a great triumph in motion now. The influx of light into the earth planet is the vibration of the descent of the consciousness for peace, the dove of light, the spirit of the consciousness of the cosmic law.

We wish to speak to each and all who have the ears to hear, and the hearts to open and the minds to access and the strength to acknowledge

The great tribulation is the release of that which has brought the human endeavors into enslaved action. The Law of Karmic Cause and Effect is in effect. The historical consciousness of human lives through generations of time has met its moment for release, resolution and peace.

Before new beginnings, the endings must occur. Before the door opens for its highest endeavors, the path must clear. You are observing the most awesome change in human direction, social direction, economic direction, materialistic direction, technical direction, ecological direction and spiritual direction. All situations addressed by the soul, with the energies of hierarchical help, is intended to enlighten the mind, the heart and the spirit.

Those who have resistance to these experiences will find themselves in confusion and denial. To those who understand, great joy, exaltation expectation comes. The dividing of the way has come into effect. You will see those who cannot hear, will not see and are blind. You will also see others who cannot take enough into themselves, whose quest in understanding grows day by day for spiritual joy.

Each and all are attractive for your gifts, your gifts of teaching, understanding, love, counsel and your gifts of light. You already are in the experience of finding yourself sought after and repelled.

The time in effect is a millennium for developments of humanity's need for dignity, honor and peace. Informational activities servicing man for emotional, mental and spiritual growth are most important. The sciences of life, regarding replenishing the earth, instill life where death seems to be in the species of many earth forms. You are going to find the present time challenging and extraordinarily rewarding.

We cannot make absolute predictions in reference to the outcome of critical forks in the road of earth's initiation. We can only speak in these terms: messages have been presented and will continue to be presented to as many ears as can hear and to as many hearts are open to initiate love. We walk with you and continue to assist you through challenge and through the clouded vision of your own ego systems.

You are most beautiful. You are angels of light to a certain extent, not in full angelic consciousness, to be sure. Nevertheless, divine sparks choosing to walk in this earth with renewed activity to serve. You serve in your home and you serve with those who are a part of your circle of life. You write and you teach, you heal and you touch, you love and you give and you openly believe without fear. You will not walk without needs met or live without the necessities for your experience. All things are added to your life as needed to facilitate your personal journey.

Beloved Ones, at this moment perceive all your fears of doubt, and self-deserve, the limited effects of your diminished ego, all this give to the light. Release this part of you and accept the merging of your inner to your outer. Experience the magnificence of your true self that cosmically knows it is a citizen of a greater universe, as well as an individual in the human family of life.

The Order of Melchizedek has sent the decree throughout the universe, through many channels, that the ending of this decade is the beginning of the inner Christ magnified individually and collectively to service the planet.

Discernment will be most difficult. Stay true to yourself, stay true to the gifts, stay true to the creative urges that direct your thoughts and initiate you into action. **Trust in the process of your own journey.**

Where eruptions take place and changes occur it brings release within for healing. Live each day as though it is the eternal moment of all you have ever been, and all you will ever be. Live each moment as though that eternal now is in the physical as well as in the spiritual. When you have the key of living in the moment, in the ever eternal now with total acceptance of your presence as sufficient for every moment of your day, you will find the peace.

I am Joshua, I have spoken before and am grateful and in gratitude for these transmitted moments of thought. Each of all of you, are one of many, who are, linked to the great change of this earth's experience.

 White, Gold & Blue

Now the pyramid magnificently created in all its many hues of light, are active by thought. As you center in the frequency of the Wisdom Ray, Gold and White in silence bring those you love.

Does Christ return as he walked the earth before as a man, or does Christ return in spirit as a ever present being of all recognized as itself as Christ. These truths you will know in your own heart. Many will say they are, *the Christ*, many will call you to find the Christ, many will speak as the Christ as one, let the Christ live in you, let yourself become The Spirit.

Key & Code 3

THE SPIRAL

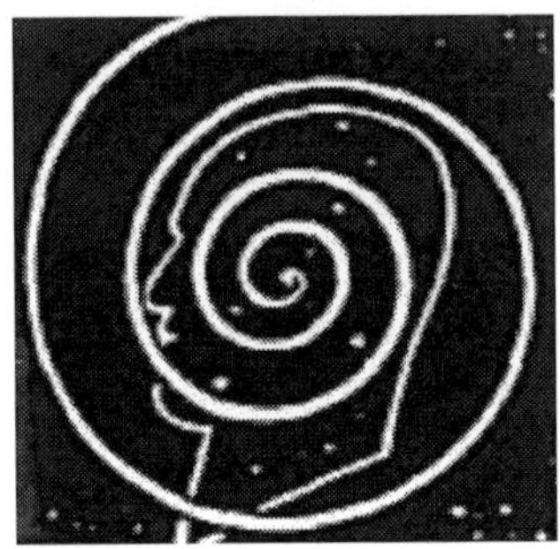

The Code is The Spiral

The Code is the Spiral that moves round and round unending, but moving always in a upward motion, until it is a consciousness that connects you to All That Is.

Universal and cosmic, this is the connecting consciousness of all universes. This is the Time Travel Code. Mind represents the power of the central core key. This represents energy in constant cycles. This symbolizes the way you travel through dimensions to the point of Light within the mind and spirit. This is the symbol of mind, and as mind expands so, it expands in a spiral effect.

The Key is the mantra:

**I AM AS MIND. I AM AS MANNA.
I AM AS LIGHT. I AM AS ENERGY.
I AM MANIFESTING.
LET THERE BE LIGHT IN ALL.**

Message #1

Within this path, we wish to introduce and activate from memory within you the symbol of The Mind and the way to The Mind of the All In All. The *All* represents the all-knowing, the all-seeing frequency acknowledged as the symbol of the, **I AM**.

This is the key that allows you to travel from physical form to dimensions of astral and soul levels through the angelic planes into monadic systems and into the Mind. These travels to the Mind enable you to meet with others who have connections with you and travels within the physical dimensions or what you call manifestations of earthly being.

I will speak very conservatively on this symbol and ask you each to just envision this. Allow yourself to move with its vibration. You can instantly connect to your body and to what you need to feel attached physically.

Let your essence move. Allow the symbol to draw your consciousness to the Light. As you are experiencing the movement of this vibrational pattern, recognize there is no limitation by dimension or formula of measurement. Again, it is a symbol of the Mind, and as the Mind expands, it moves in a spiral effect. Hold this as a symbol of the race mind of the soul's journey through its own evolving being, where the race of man has been in the will of its own karmic patterns. Visually hold this image upon those particular places in which you find races of thought in karmic cycles of repetition manifestations. Perceive this as a vibrational system of thought affecting opportunity to move beyond the limitations of hate, rage and pain. Let it be seen, as a way in which thought rises through the spiral and human consciousness to its point of truth and Light where you feel in the heart the pain of patterns of rage, ask to:

SEE WHAT YOU KNOW.
KNOW WHAT YOU SEE.

Now say

I AM AS MIND, I AM AS MANNA.
I AM AS LIGHT. I AM AS ENERGY.
I AM MANIFESTING.
LET THERE BE LIGHT IN ALL.

Place this experience of light around those experiences of karmic reactions. You are called to gather for the purpose of manifest ting self directed spiritual love and Light. Always know you are sending an opportunity for response. You cannot change the patterns through the power of light if you hold self-judgment. You must hold the pattern or idea, as a loving key presented without expectation, yet knowing the vibration is empowered without expectation and is empowered with the spirit of love and truth.

When you return to your body and you feel yourself moving through denser and denser levels, do not resist your body and who you are, welcome your physical, embrace it with love. See your self in balance, in hope, wisdom and truth. And so it is.

In the past, there was much ritual with those experiences but there is beauty in the simplicity and beauty in the simple act of presenting yourself as you are. Walk now with peace.

Message #2

The Council of Light greets each of you and all those who have yet to appear, and are prepared inwardly for this step into new consciousness. I am the teacher, Annanius;

In this moment, there is a review and a key activated for you is the key of traveling of time. This is the path of Light bringing you into and through different dimensions of consciousness.

While we can speak certain words, they are limited. Your consciousness is in individual realities. What you will sense is the spiral of light connecting you to the inner dimensions which link you to all the many myriad lives you have lived before. There is but one life and all lives are but one life. Present and future are all apart of one. The present is both the past and the future in its time of what you see, where you live in consciousness. However, time travel is the freedom to be unlimited by the boundaries of your conscious thoughts.

So, let the self be uplifted to where you desire to discover what is for you to see. You will move up and into the spiral of the Light. Some see it as stairways and others as circles of energy that moves you through and into many dimensions of Light. You are both; all of your past and you are the future becoming. You are the present as you have attained connections to what you are and what you are to be and the shift in consciousness for the planet is relative to what you are expressing. Let go of limitation and let go of analyzing. Just except what is

In this spiral of Light, you can be at any place at any time, you can see the history of what was or you can be in another place observing someone you know or those yet to be met. In this spiral of Light in time travel of the soul, you are directed by thoughts and intentions within you. You can see your past, you can see your future and only what you need to know is what you will discover.

What you must know above all else is, death is the illusion, infinity is the recognition that nothing ends; *it transforms*. Change is but a shift in all physical, mental, emotional and spiritual parts of you. In the angelic realms and beyond there is no past; no future there is only life becoming a constant state of creation from The Mind governing all things. In the angelic realm, you will sense and see you are part of something bigger then anything, it is perfect.

To experience this in all-ness is difficult to absorb. Practice as you come together to initiate time travel and work with healing in ways you have never done before. By thought, seeing, feeling and knowing your presence, you travel to any place you are required. Others will see you in dream states and you will be working with many, who will never see you in this physical world, but you are their guardians in this time and it is good.

The Code is the Spiral that moves round and round unending, but moving always in a upward motion, until it is a consciousness that connects you to All That Is.

The time travel is the key number 3 and relates to the Wisdom Light. It connects with the Silver Cord and brings you up and through levels of space and travel. The cord always is connected to the soul and will never be broken, as long as you accept you desire to live within your body. Many unusual experiences come with this key; it can be extremely experiential for the healing of others by The Mind and from a higher perspective.

When you are ready, draw yourself back. You will find it very difficult for your desire to draw you back, for you recognize you were in such peace, in such a lightness of being, but do know you can bring this lightness through and into you so the body that you live in will feel more balanced.

Draw your energy back and let your consciousness flow, moving back into all that you are physically and until your consciousness moves into and through everything physically.

When you are ready anchor your thoughts and energy down through your feet and feel yourself settling within the physical body.

41

Know that many things have shifted from this journey. Walk in peace my students, walk in peace each of you. You each have been so important in the consciousness of the Order of Melchizedek and there is much yet to experience and manifest in your individual lives. Go in peace.

Lesson Four

COLOR RAY: EMERALD GREEN

The Light of Creativity

Activate the Meditation Procedure

Message & Meditation #1

The greatest lesson you now experience, is freeing yourself from conflicts you carry within you as a necessary part of your lesson learning experience. Release the guilt of not being perfect. The perfection you seek to project is an illusion. Recognize this. Once you understand perfection, as you know it an illusion, you will free yourself from the fear of being imperfect. The soul existing in each person within the earth is an imperfect soul. The soul, if it were in its perfected state, would not need to leave the source of perfection. It would remain within the envelopment of the Creator itself.

I, Andrew, who has existed on many different levels of time and space, have known what it is to search and to meet the one idea of perfection, but never have achieved that total source of my own being. If I Andrew, at this level of consciousness is less than a perfected entity, then you as a physical human self cannot expect perfection within yourself. Earth life is not a path in which everything is in its perfect state; it is a path of creating different means of developing ways to see a perfected self. It is a means of humans coming to different terms of what perfection is.

At this moment, we are going to activate the vibrations of energy within the body to transmute the holding on to mental images of imperfection and perfection. Resolve in this time, *you are as you were meant to be.* You are a perfect being in regards to how it seems to others, to life and to yourself. You see, it is a dichotomy -- while you affirm the perfection, it is a perfection of spirit translated into a physical life. Your life <u>is</u> a perfect consciousness that exists as *it is meant to be.* When the egos of the physical body begin to fight and resist the idea of being worthy body signals of neglect, rejection, turmoil and conflict can appear.

At this moment, perceive once again the releasing of all holding patterns of guilt that keep the body in states of tension and stress. Acknowledge the love present within you is pouring forth from you to all who can receive. This is what you come to understand, you are a loving expression and your love gives and receives exactly as spirit directs you. Love is all there is and all you came to know.

In your work and where you place your life is a source of daily challenge, but the challenges will evolve into a state of self-assurance and realization when you know you are flowing in right action.

We are now going to activate this Emerald Ray throughout all of the neck and the throat area. Perceive that you are breaking the bonds of self-imposed limitation as well as the projections of others. Affirm that you are putting into motion creative energy that will resolve the imbalances and blockages and create a secure foundation for your individual life.

Focus at this moment upon the energy and see it as a sphere of light. This sphere is enclosing and encompassing this heavy mass of conditioned thought. See it now dissipating in the vibrations of energy and affirm that you are in harmony and balance with all that life has to give.

In the name of the Christ, all things are in their perfect order. Changes come to you through your acceptance of the creative self and seeing yourself as free. By setting yourself free, you are beginning to accept there is a place for you in this scheme of life. Trust this in instinct, knowing and guidance.

Your sense life does not move as quickly as you desire it and this is a difficult lesson. Trust in the now, everything is accelerated, as you are ready to accept yourself. Nothing is withheld from you that you do not want to be withheld.

If there is one desire the hierarchy seeks to have manifested in the now, it is the desire of the human self to truly acknowledge its being one with the Creator. Not a Creator wrathful, or destructive, but The Creator that brings the flow of love into manifestation. We have spoken upon Yahweh and Jehovah, and these are aspects of the One Creator. There are many different aspects known as The Creator. Each one is a particular identity that comes to humanity during certain times. The overseer of this particular age has not yet come to knowledge within the human mind; we do not have a name for it yet.

Message & Meditation #2

It is important to assist yourself in an opportunity of hearing and becoming awakened to the visions of the next stage of your development. I, Joshua, continue to bring forth the perspective that we sense is in effect for the next generation.

You stand on the fork of a road within the consciousness of the human race. This fork is a turning point, an acceleration, for evolution, individually and planetary wise. This fork in the road is a spiritual impulse to attune to the next phase of karmic healing and of rejuvenation of consciousness. The appearance of this fork in the road will take form in the manner of social and economic developments.

What is perceived, as criteria for defense mechanisms for human life, will be placed in a different perspective. Rather than defending territories, ideologies with the power to destroy, there will be a sense of reaching for new ways to create a purpose, a destiny for human experiences. Focus will be on the healing of the planet rather than the abandoning of the planet and the total destruction of its body.

Again, predictability is based upon the flow, which comes as unified consciousness. There are always those diverse realities that can change the balance of the scale, so to speak. As more strive for individual choice for living in accordance with personal needs there will be less boundaries placed upon the individual self. These goals are most important as spirit and soul come into effect in the human journey.

You will also see others who cannot accept these realities and continue in their blindness and pain. You are the links for understanding, for gifts of healing and for the opportunity for sight and sound to be recognized as spiritual truth.

In the past, you have worked within yourself to understand the composite of who you are and the many aspects of your nature attuned to past journeys of the earth. The next decade is recognizing your composite as a complete and a whole person that forges toward a new future.

The economic picture will change, and become a value system based upon stronger equality. The struggle through this will be difficult for many. Be assured, as you hold fast to your own understanding of yourself and your place in the plan, your needs will come together to assist and develop your personal evolution.

Planetary Light Work

Each and all of you beautiful ones come together, unified as a group. Perceive your spark, your divinity with light, one with many. Perceive the vibrations of your consciousness shared as beings of light and know that you work together with others of other planes who also seek to intervene in the destructive tendencies. See the planet, and all of those struggling to free themselves from resistance, being in light. Envision the communication breaking through walls of misunderstanding; opening to the one truth that each and all are light.

See the earth itself in a great pyramid of energy, in a magnetic field so vast the earth as a planet in enveloped in strains, bands, waves and frequencies of light. Know this envisioned thought is a manifestation attuned to hierarchical intent from all the schools of the past held in the mysteries of consciousness. There are those visionaries who have held threads of wisdom and truth in consciousness and have foreseen patterns of evolution. Now the brink to a threshold of change is in your vision. What you see for the planet, you individualize for your own expression.

When you have completed your experience, acknowledge yourself accepting the reality of your body, your connection to the earth and the lessons of your individual self. With this acceptance, perceive your rightful balance. Go in peace.

Key & Code 4

THE STAR OF DAVID

The Code is The Star of David

The circle represents the cycles of the Alpha and Omega, the beginning and the end, the end and the beginning as one.

The triangle pointing downward of the Star of David represents the consciousness of the Council's Mind, the Creator's Mind, the God-self Mind, Universal Mind and the encompassing consciousness of higher realities earthed into conscious acceptance into matter.   The triangle pointing upward represents your conscious seeking to reach a state of interrelationship with worlds beyond and universes beyond.

The Key is the mantra:

**I SEE WHAT I KNOW.
I AM IN MY KNOWING AND MY SEEING.
I ACCEPT WITHOUT QUESTION.
I AM AT PEACE.**

We see you with great joy and Light. Your heart as soul is open to respond to the procedures directing your path to the higher kingdoms of Light.

Each of the keys you are responding too, are being developed for your evolving self and for the service you are rendering for the planet's change. All of this brings your conscious self and your inner spirit to a moment where unification transpires.

I am bringing you out of these lower kingdoms into the gateways to the inner planes where your familiar self can meet with those in council who have governed many of the states of activities of all universes in motion.

It is difficult for intellect to connect to the rhyme and reason for what we bring and present. Once again the intellect must take a seat and release its logical relation to its physical dimension, and open to a higher self that understands and remembers itself in these other forms of being.

First, activate the Eye. If you could know all that you see and could see all that you know, your all-knowingness would have all things in perfect understanding.

Intellect cannot absorb the all-knowing, it must decipher through its familiar path of logic and reason, experience and conscious development.

Say:

I SEE WHAT I KNOW.
I AM IN MY KNOWING AND MY SEEING.
I ACCEPT WITHOUT QUESTION.
I AM AT PEACE.

The key introduced is the familiar symbol known as the Star of David. The Star of David represents the consciousness of the Council's Mind, the Creator's Mind, the God-Self Mind, the Universal Mind and the encompassing consciousness of higher realities earthed into conscious acceptance and into matter.

The lower triangle represents you, the initiate, the neophyte, the seeker, the pilgrim, the way-shower, the light bearer and the earthed soul in cycles of growth. It represents your consciousness seeking to reach a state of interrelationship with that which lies beyond, worlds beyond and universes beyond.

Focus now and expand the Star of David until you are a center within it. The energy of the Emerald Ray moves in a circle in and around this interlocking triangulation of Light. You may see it in many hues of color.

This symbol known to tribes imprinted in crests and heroic shields is the symbol representing tribes of Israel, or those who come from the gods of light. It is also representing the energy most naturally seen within your soul pattern. In the meditation, accept this symbol protects, interrelates and interlocks your consciousness with wisdom, knowledge and truth. It belongs to no particular race of man, but is the symbol of those who come forth from the tribes of Melchizedek governed by the many lords of light, Azreal and Ishmael.

This symbol can be a protecting shield and directed by thought to balance conflict rising out of fear, judgment, foolishness and illusion. When doubt comes to mind and conflict rises to the experiences in life, place this shield upon the energy of the moment and see it come to its balanced state, a karmically perfected state of being.

Many of you will begin to see within the Star of David many triangles like diamonds and pyramids, each in hues of color of different frequency rays as though you were looking in multidimensional facets of light. This too represents codes and keys of the universe; the interlocking light forms, representing creative thought, ideas and spirit.

As you are focused within observe how the body and all that you are begins to harmonize to ease out of its constriction, to break the patterns of pain, to unlock and unblock the power within.

Some of you will begin to observe that this spins, moves and flows. There can be no time limit directed to you. Only your consciousness can know its time to return to its own physical self. We direct you to live, move and have your being within this consciousness.

In your completion, you will discover new realities of your own thoughts. You are most beloved. We are pleased. This work is not to be limited by anyone, but collectively developed, to be explored and experienced by all who are recognizing time changes, life changes and preparations for transitional changes. Lord Michael and Azreal speak with you and guide the path. And so it is.

Lesson Five

COLOR RAY: VIOLET-PURPLE

The Light of the Will

Activate the meditation procedure

Message & Meditation #1

Once again, be lifted up through the Rainbow Bridge and connect to the consciousness within the planetary center. Go deep into the silence, commune with the guides, teachers and masters. Magnify the Violet-Purple Ray. Now perceive energy directed through the networking of Light and into the earth, releasing the vibrant energy into all consciousness. This vibration brings forth good will into the minds and hearts of individuals. Perceive this energy directed towards all who are open to receive its essence in their consciousness to change the course of ill-will rage to love, angers and hostilities to joy and war into alignment, unity and peace.

Message #1

This is Andrew

Here within the planetary center, envelop self in the vibration of the masters and teachers of the hierarchy, remember within this plateau of consciousness, all thoughts become as a resounding vibration. Trust your lives are being focused, into an acceleration internally, so that the outer plane may begin to create its right action.

We know each of you came into a very intense time for re-conditioning yourself. Your outer lives are changing very dramatically to accommodate the difficulties of your path, but know each one of you will find the key that unlocks the door of repressed activity and freeing you to explore the greater joys you have always known there would be.

At this point, experience the inner Divine Spirit, which governs your own particular path. It is time to flow with the consciousness and guidance that stems from your own personal aspect.

You have come through many phases of self-denial to a place in which faith is a very strong cord pushing you forward into higher stages of conscious knowing. Through the lessons of Light, each one release old elements of striving to break the barriers through of forces and release the controlling element into Inner Divine Will.

Do not be discouraged by those who feel a disillusionment regarding personal growth. The path is very diverse and filled with many obstacles. Each one will come to that point of inner knowing through their Divine Spirit. All will move through their path in an individual pace to face their own inner, as well as the outer consciousness.

Your egos are aware of the many vibrant colors and beams of light. As you direct the energy out through the networks, perceive them once again as being a force for upliftment, for cleansing and for transmuting. Let your egos travel through these frequencies to places calling your own spirit. Your light is magnifying the evolutionary stages of all human development and all human consciousness. Flow into those areas to which you are drawn. Perceive them as dissipating the counter-evolutionary forces.

The battles are strong. Perceive you are individual working singularly, as well a part of a wave of many higher beings who uplift your own consciousness. Flow with your light to those who are in need of release from pain, sorrow and hunger.

Let go of personal responsibility regarding the effects of the light. Perceive each one given according to their particular needed experience. It is important to understand those who seek fulfillment walk through their own phases of self-denial in order to awaken into light. This denial aspect is the most prominent resistant force to one's true consciousness. As collective thought has a most forceful impact upon the conscious minds of individuals, it takes the strength of all of one's faith to break through those negative conditionings.

Perceive the earth, the planet, enveloped in a rainbow of light. Perceive the outer aura as transmuted from the muddied and darkened element. It is difficult to see this, for the denseness is like a crystallized, negative electrical force. For the networks of light to break through these barriers, it takes the mind of the higher self to oversee all of the negatives with a tremendous degree of energy.

Perceive the rainbow as a vibrant clearing, moving faster than sound. Perceive the light as exploding the consciousness of self-destruction and clearing pathways for those individuals who are feeling the impact of new awakenings. Many are experiencing higher frequencies without a conscious understanding of what is transpiring within the physical senses.

As light bearers, you are the guiding instruments to help those who are confused by the pressures within their bodies and the strange sensations that occur within their physical selves.

As you feel their confusion, know they are in new stage of self-awakening. The great awakening takes place regardless of race or color. It is sweeping through the human mind to those who are ready to put aside all of the self-destructive aspects that keep them bound in karmic wheels.

The great awakening, as prophesied in the past, is coming into a tremendous new force. This is all part of the transforming of human, as well as planetary consciousness. It is difficult for the conscious ego to truly perceive the impact of the light, for the denseness of matter seems to be so opposing to the intangible consciousness of a higher attunement. Beloved ones, this is a path that leads you to that point of true integration of all of your higher being.

The peace felt in the inner planes far surpasses any consciousness known in your physical world. Yet, is important you function in the physical, bringing that heightened expression of total tranquility into this plane of physical existence. As you become released from the ego's desires, caught in webs of its own making, you begin to sense more tranquility through all parts of your life.

You have free will to choose what you truly desire and need for your present individual experiences. Use your tools of light and feel the flow of unity, peace and harmony throughout your own consciousness.

Now perceive that with the birth of the inner-Christ recognized within, you are renewed and moved forward with understanding and joy. Give your gifts without fear. Give your gifts with love.

 White, Gold and Silver, Emerald Green, Violet Purple and Blue

As you return to your own centers, move back down through the Rainbow Bridge of Light, re-activating the pyramidal structures of energy. Feel the magnetic field released from any negative vibrations, and feel the essence of the White, Gold and Silver, Emerald Green, Violet-Purple and the Blue Wisdom Ray, all magnified in triangles of light. Let the higher self guide this frequency into its perfect pattern. This is another energy system that creates the inner work necessary for balancing, blending and integrating the inner self with the outer expression.

Message #2

I am Joshua. I have spoken before. I am grateful and in gratitude for these transmitted moments of thought. Each and all of you are one of many linked to the great change of this earth's experience.

The pyramids of light are activated by your thought, by your being and can be magnificently created in all its many hues of light, but you are centered mostly in the frequency of the Wisdom ray, and Golden-White encompasses you. Be in the silence in this pyramid structure as though it is a place of your personal, joyful moment in love.

Some have asked, *"Does Christ return as He walked the earth before, as a man?   Or does Christ return in spirit, as an ever present being of all who recognize itself as Christ?"*

These truths you will know within your own heart. Many will say they are, the Christ. Many will call you to find the Christ. Many will speak of the Christ as one. Let the Christ live in you. Let you become the spirit.

From the author ...

When Joshua first channeled through me an incredible phenomena took place.

It was just after New Years day and I had taken down the Christmas decorations. As I was putting them away, I heard a voice say to me, "leave the lights on the little tree." The tree was by the fireplace. So, I left the Christmas tree lights on the tree.

That night the class arrived for their meditation and lessons of the A Course in Light. During the Joshua channeling the lights on the tree started to blink on and off. This was not a blinking set of lights. As I open my eyes, I saw the lights blinking and everyone was staring at them. About a minute or two later they stopped blinking and went back to their normal steady White Light. Since then, I have always felt strong powerful energy from Joshua.

 Create your own pyramid.

Perceive this structure of light expanded to 150 feet. Call those who are in your lives, relationships, associations, and friendships. Bring them into this pyramid of light for cleansing and healing. Ask each one who is connected to your vibration be given the perfect lessons in their own life expression and that there is healing resolving all unfinished business.

Ground your energies through the body, down through the legs and out the feet into The Black Power Ray.

Key & Code 5

THE LOTUS

The Code is The Lotus

The interlocking of many beliefs, understanding and truisms for a multi-faceted perception is an image of a perfect flower, The Lotus.   The opening of this symbol brings into effect many changes.

The Key is the mantra:

**THE MANY AS ONE,
ARE WORLDS WITHIN.
ALL WORLDS AS ONE
CREATE THE LIGHT AND LIFE.
THE MANY WORLDS ARE ONE.**

We speak for The Council concerning the messages needed for earth development.   Much has transpired through the coming together of those who assist in the evolving life path of the families of the earth and those of other planes.

The key for this particular lesson is a coded key you have seen many times, referred in ancient wisdom as the Lotus.

The many petals of a Lotus flower are a design representing the interlocking of many beliefs, understanding and truisms. The form of a multi-faceted perfect flower is The Code. The opening of this symbol brings many changes in your individual self and others through the Higher Will.

The Key is:

THE MANY WORLDS ARE ONE.
THE MANY AS ONE,
ARE WORLDS WITHIN.
ALL WORLDS AS ONE,
CREATE THE LIGHT AND LIFE.

The Mandela is The Lotus

Focus now on the center of your will receiving this Key and Code of Consciousness. See yourself as a representative of your world, ready to meet those in other planes, in other places and in other states of being.

Each key is in its time, in perfect order with your evolving self. The keys cannot take away your challenge. They allow you to meet your challenge with more openness of thought, a greater inner strength, with wisdom and trust.

The Mandela, the Lotus, has always been perceived as a sacred sign representing healing, power, the interlocking connection between the physical world and the spiritual path, the way of the peaceful warrior by the its inner- most strength.

Let the silence continue. The ceremony is complete within its own individual experience.

From the Author …

Each, focus your thoughts and awareness bringing your egos into the forebrain. Release all that has cluttered your thoughts, your mind has created from the business of the week.

Now bring into the forebrain the personality ego, the physical body ego, the organic and cellular egos and we bring into the forebrain the ego of our higher self or soul. As all of the egos are centered within this place begin your breathing. Breathe in and move with your breath through your body until your body finds your rhythm and the body becomes very still and with each and all egos focused. We are going to direct them to the star center above your head.

Often as we are in this center we see this as our special place, communication center and within this place, we invite our teachers, our guides and our special masters of the Order of Melchizedek. And with this process of bringing you to this place, thinking of your self releasing all conditionings within your self, just let go of what you think of what you should be doing and just know that you are in your right opportunities, just as they are. Go into a very deep level of personal meditation.

Meditation & Message

Azreal

This is Azreal speaking to each and all, bringing the lesson of this time **"manifestations for the fulfillment of intent"** to you personal opportunities. The lessons of this come to you in many different demonstrations.

You are each capable of creating your own personal intention and design, which comes from your own higher selves.

So in this moment, as we observe, each of you are struggling through the understanding of what is meant for you to do. We tell you beloved ones, let go of the struggle, let go of thinking; feeling and perceiving you are in opposition to your own intent. Your journey takes you through the lessons meant for you. As you step to the plate as you so call it, with an open mind, an open heart, you are exploring the highest vibration meant for you to transmit to the planet earth.

So, we are going to activate a key, the key of the code of consciousness manifesting higher will through you. The key of this code of consciousness is relative to patterns of Light perceived geometrically as a lotus blossom. Like the many petals of a Lotus, there are many aspects of you, each relative to a special purpose of your highest goal.

Visually perceive as we speak, you are in a place relative to a spiritual design, in a plateau of Light. Within this plateau of energy, you are coded with this vibration of the Lotus and its many petals. They represent the phases of you and your opportunities to unfold your spiritual design. Some of you will see colors relative to the Violet Purple and all the hues that are associated with this center. Others will see as though this pattern of energy is in many colors, multi-facetted each representing a specific gift, a specific intent of your many selves. Do not try to intellectualize what we bring to you; simply be in the moment as we bring this through. So the key is the key relative to the will center of you.

This is similar to the *Flower of Life*[2] pattern. It is a geometrical system of energy. It is associated with dimensions of you that are a part of the higher self and beyond. So in this design of Light just experience what transpires and key words are the will of the father/mother, the will of the higher self, the will of soul intent, the will of that which is the karmic balance, the wheel of full living in the Light.

Know you have the will to create your intent, your purpose, your design and your essence. Know that in the soul Light this magnification of soul energy is in place.

In ancient days under the sacred orders of mystery schools, frequently a sign was activated in this center of the will. It was a protection against anyone else's power. Today, this is relative to being connected inner dimensionally. As we speak, know you are standing before your master teachers who activate and present this consciousness with you. In your language, the word surrender has always been associated with giving up the power of your will. However, this is surrendering to what is beyond you. It is integration, it is integrating a higher consciousness of Light that is connecting to the many selves of you and awakening at the level of your egos the perfect destiny of your soul.

The many petals are what you perceive as the design of the Lotus in bloom, symbolic to the many aspects of you fully open to the divine energy connected with you for your highest good. With this magnified energy, whatever ill will exists, whatever pain carried forward into this life, it is being dissipated. With this vibration in full activation, you can never harbor the ill winds of revenge nor perceive yourself to be submissive to negative powers outside of you. When this activation is in full expression, find yourself in

---

[2] Drunvalo Melchizedek workshops

peace with what you know as all the purposes you came to fulfill and they are good.

Whatever ill winds have come forward into your path, whatever challenges and suffering have been apart of your experience, whatever conditions have created the struggles of your ego, each and all are manifestations of lessons. So, accept and know it is all divine and you have achieved a state of release of its hold on you. There is no power outside of you that can stand in the Light of this consciousness. Know this to be so and hold it deep within and so it is.

The activation of this code of consciousness is magnified within the center of The Will. It expands until all that is a part of you is experiencing itself as a Radiant Vibrant Violet Ray of Light. You are in the will of the father/mother self.

You have all passed through extreme tests of your personal will. You have each passed through conditions that were challenging to you. You have each walked through the fire of fear and met the passion of anger. You have each faced the shadowed self and now stand complete with a higher will integrating through you and centering itself within you.

Some of the results of the activation of this key are the ability to be more sensitive to other dimensions, seeing, feeling and knowing the communications given by your masters and those on the other side. So do not fear, let it be.

The lessons of your individual work will continue in their order but this beloved students, is of a higher system and you will each find your own personal relation to what is given. Because the earth is in its shifting time, you are accelerated into your ascension process. Go in peace and release all self-doubt and so it is.

Lesson Six

COLOR RAY: RUBY RED

The Left Hand of the Physician

Activate the meditation procedure

Message & Meditation #1

Greetings, students of light, this is Azreal.

We speak with the Light of your inner being and through the consciousness of your higher self; you will experience the activity of light through every phase of your expression.

Come into the element of the temples to experience a moment of silence and the communion with the masters and teachers of your own consciousness.

 Merge with the Council of Light, affirm your purpose and desire to bring forth the highest good through every activity of your personal, individual experience, re-affirming the divine design of your own soul activity.

You are experiencing an elevation of all selves into the consciousness of light. You are experiencing openness, movement and the magnification of your individualized highest self.

The Christ is manifesting and bringing into effect all of those who can see the way of greater good coming into fruition through this time frame. The time of integration and elevation is at hand. All of you have difficulties in your personal lives, yet are finding love within the source of your highest consciousness. All of you are experiencing moments when you are in states of inner joy and tranquility when you see a greater plan is manifesting through your life.

As you release intimidations and concepts of being bound physically, you are directing your higher self through the physical and becoming an instrument for the light.

The process of your self-awakening is through many stages of awareness and non-awareness. Therefore, you are the practicing lightworkers as you accept this. No one should interfere in your creative expression. No system should block the process of your upliftment and light.

Don't give energy to conditions that stand in the way of your higher will. Emphasize through collective thought, the highest good and know you are emerging as true teachers and practicing energizers of higher awareness. As you emanate light, you uplift and clear the lower planes.

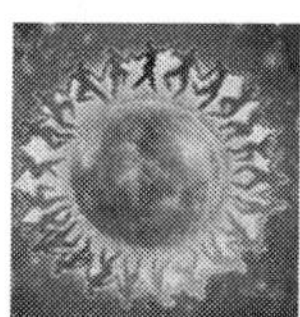

As you perceive the physical world moving through a shift in consciousness, the planet moving into a new vibration, see the human elements of confusion, fear, hostility and in separateness bathed in the Radiant Ruby Red Light. Visualize the essence of the Radiant Ruby Red Light; move in and throughout the networking of consciousness into the human egos, into the planet earth and the auras that emanate from its vibration. The human mental plane is a collective vibration of many karmic embattlements.

Again, mass-mind perceives its earth as its only source of expression. Yet, you know there are many planes and systems of Mind. See now the impact of light clearing the imageries of distortion. Focus on the vibration of this frequency of light dissipating all false-to-fact elements within the mental and perceptual aspects.

You desire to know what the future holds, what do the masters see as manifesting. We perceive the forces that would deny the free aspect of human consciousness as coming into a tremendous power. We also perceive that many of the enlightened ones are creating centers of light, vortices of energy for working from the inner planes to the outer, in order to awaken the human ego to its evolution into its new system of expression.

The warring factors within individual systems will be the manifestation of dis-ease in individual lives. Therefore, release, know and affirm that you are one with the Christ or Cosmic Consciousness. Affirm that you are creating avenues for perfected growth.

As the planet shifts in consciousness, there will be certain shifts in the physical plane, but we do not perceive the destruction envisioned by the prophets of old. We perceive an activity of change in certain parts of the earth; in Japan, in Asia, and in certain European aspects. But for the greater whole, we sense that through the Christed aspect will come a new wave of human expression of unifying and of new hope. We do not perceive the destructiveness of the earth planet. We perceive the dissipating of the intensity of the warring factors. Trust. Create an inner peace within self and the outer world will reflect what you have put into motion through your mind, your higher consciousness.

It is time to rejoice; it is time to see there is a period of manifestation that is now coming into order. It is time to let go of separateness, pain and the angers of self-denial.

Perceive there is an over-element of higher consciousness that is breaking through the barriers. It is time to be individually a strong force of consciousness of light. It is time to be integrated, open, clear and functioning with a sense of order, a sense of perfection and with a sense of being an instrument, a communicator, and a voice for higher will.

Be emphatic on your purpose.
Be emphatic on your destiny.
Be emphatic on the design your soul

As light workers and disciples within the earth, envelop your consciousness with the will of the higher masters, the angels of light, the thought adjusters and the activators of the greater good. Walk with light; walk with strength. Be true to self. Let the integrity of your higher will come forth in all actions.

Blessings unto you

Key & Code 6

THE CROSS & HEART & ROSE

The Code is The Cross, Heart & Rose

The Heart represents the soul's desire.

The Cross, represents a balanced law of cause and effect, "the karmic Cross of release."

The Rose represents the perfect image of Christ Consciousness or Spirit as Love.

The Key is:

WITHIN THE DESIRE OF THE HEART
OF WHO I AM,
I SURRENDER THE WILL OF MY BEING,
TO THE KARMIC CROSS OF RELEASE.

Message #1

It is good to move with you through time, light, spirit and mind. We are presenting the consciousness that is most extraordinary for your changes of being. The key to the heart is love. The representation of love is through the rose. The way to freedom from all the pain the heart holds is by the cross.

Therefore, we ask you to focus and meditate on this mantra:

**I ACCEPT THE VIBRATION OF LOVE LIKE A ROSE
TO HEAL ALL THAT IS WITHIN THE DESIRE
OF THE HEART OF WHO I AM,
I SURRENDER THE WILL OF MY BEING
TO THE KARMIC CROSS OF RELEASE.**

The Heart bears the cross of pain, the Heart carries the cross and burdens of concern. The heart remembers the lack of love and holds in its own being the impressions of all that has denied love. The heart becomes weak when it is without release. The heart can manifest out of its pain, the rages of its inner cry. The heart longs for the reflection of its innermost self. The heart desires to share its own being as love with one who reflects and mirrors its image in return.

The source of the Heart is the soul and the soul as Heart seeks its own design. It reaches to touch and draw to itself what it desires to relay, but the pain of the past, the memories of things undone, shield the heart from its true Light.

Through the Keys and Codes of Consciousness, focus on the cross as though you are bringing into the cross all that has been heavy in the cells, all that has been difficult to bear, all that has been an experience of grieving the losses of love.

Place upon the Cross all your needs, hurts and pain and visualize the Cross as an energy field about you, in front of you, even placed at your feet where you can walk upon it or stand on it. This is the symbol of crossing out the past, the burdens and the negations of the heart. You can live in freedom. You can be free.

The Rose is the gift and symbol of love from the highest source of being, from The Christ, as in Jesus Christ. Hold this in your heart, and know you step into a new consciousness of being healed of the wounds, the rage and the loss.

Message #2

Azreal

The gift of love is yours to accept, to experience as a completion of all the pain from the lives of many unsavory directions.

I am Azreal coming to you again with love to heal the hearts, to bring you into openness, to explore the clarity of your true self. I come to bring you into acceptance that you can walk through the paths with new lives, with new openness to accept and become free, to live by the Keys and Codes of your inner most self.

You are in the Light radiating from a center in all the hues of energy. We are bringing forth the vibration of the Karmic Cross of Release. This comes to you as a radiant magnetic field of Light. The hues within are the pure color of White. The cross, beloved ones, is the symbol, which completes the cycles of karma. This is the Karmic Cross of Release. Here you present the hearts' burdens, holding you as your cross of heaviness of fear.

This is the Karmic Cross. Freely you are able to surrender the will of all the desires of your consciousness to this Karmic Cross. You can be healed from heaviness such as sorrow and fears of life.

In its radiance, perceive its magnificence and see your self, centered in a field of Light of this radiant cross of energy. This coded cross has always been with you, has always been a part of you; it shall become a greater understanding within you.

This Cross, when in activation, becomes a burning emblem of energy. The fire consumes what is needed to be in total release. We ask you now to open, to accept your ability to represent to the cross all you wish released and healed. Speak the words from your heart.

**I ACCEPT THE VIBRATION OF LOVE LIKE A ROSE
TO HEAL ALL THAT IS WITHIN THE DESIRE
OF THE HEART OF WHO I AM,
I SURRENDER THE WILL OF MY BEING
TO THE KARMIC CROSS OF RELEASE.**

Surrender the judgments of the past, surrender the fear of choice, surrender the resistances to your understanding and surrender the willfulness of your own desires to the Karmic Cross of Release.

See the beautiful Radiant Heart, the symbol of the encompassing love of divine energy, magnified and all in need of healing brought to the Heart of Light. Perceive this healing presented to you as a rose and this radiant rose becomes your inner symbol of divine love and perfection within your heart, within your essence.

Though the heart has borne the pain of all that you have held on to, the energy of love consumes the pain and brings into you a healing.

Each moment you experience this particular key and explore this process of release, you are enveloped in the consciousness of divine love. This is the divine key, the universal key cosmically recognized as the key connecting you to the Cosmic Christ, Christ incarnate, the Lord Christ, Jesus the Christ.

This symbol links you to the Divine Mind, Spirit and Soul to the Cosmic Order and the Law of Divine Love. This key frees you from all that has been in pain.

Your time with this symbol is your own. Your acceptance of this symbol is your choice. Your own experience of this symbol is your release. And so it is.

Lesson Seven

COLOR RAY: ORANGE

The Right Hand of the Physician

Perception & Sensitivity

Activate the meditation procedure

Message & Meditation #1

Andrew

It is so good to connect with each of you and to all those who follow in this experience of light.

Perception is the natural state of seeing. It is not the outer eye; it is the inner eye that perceives. The outer eye responds to what it registers as truth. The inner eye receives pulses of vibrations that stimulate and quicken certain instinctive consciousness within self. Perception is cleared of distorted thoughts, released of negative energy within the emotional self and released of judgments of misconceived and perceived ideas, as the Radiant Orange Ray magnifies.

One's inner eye can be more clearly a tool for guiding desires and objectives when the inner eye is opened and responsive to frequencies of light, sound, color and patterns. One is observant of another world when the instinctive self responds as a natural consciousness.   The communication with the psychic sense is renewed.   Perception has always been the natural tool of understanding of the soul. Soul speaks the language to perception through feelings, pictures or thoughts. At this moment, experience a connection being activated to increase your perception as your instinctive self.

Gifted perception interpreted by thought is often experienced as clairaudient or clairvoyant, through hearing or seeing.

Expanded sensitivity is a usage of this perception as a normal way of seeing, hearing and responding. For clear perception, wise thoughts, emotional stability and inner strength is required.

Perception distorted by judgments can be detrimental to others who ask for council. Unless council is given without judgment and by love it is best for the client to follow the perception of one's own inner self.

You can connect to your guidance more clearly through practice of perception. You cannot force perception into existence. You must awaken to it by releasing self-doubt and fear, by releasing resistance and distortions.

So now, beloved ones and all who follow this path, as you experience the touch of your guidance and the clearing of perceptual consciousness, be in gratitude and peace with this experience of light.

 Gold, Green and Orange

Create a pyramid of Gold, Emerald Green and Orange. Go deep into silence.

As your own perception is developed and magnified, feel yourself connected to the planet earth with a perception of the earth in radiant hues of Green, Gold and Orange. Hold each and all nations individually as strong nations unified by Higher Consciousness.

As you gradually come back into your own body, perceive yourself grounded and reaffirm your inner strength, your clarity and your freedom.

Go in peace.

Key & Code 7

THE FACES

The Code is The Faces

Perspective is the key and perspective is the imaged Light of God, the imaged Light of Yahweh, the imaged Light of Spirit and the imaged Light of all that is beyond the worlds and universes of your own reality.

The key is the many Faces and the many bodies, the multi-faces and the multi-bodies. Some would call this a totem pole; others would see it as many different bodies intermingled into one or many Faces of one.

The Key is the mantra:

**I AM IN THE REALITY OF EARTH
AND SPIRIT AS ONE.
I AM WITHOUT ILLUSION.**

Message #1

Isis

It is I, Isis speaking through The Mind and heart connecting with each and all who respond to the experience of their spiritual growth.

Initiations have always presented the initiate with challenges to the next plateau of self-manifestation. The initiate on the path of initiation often meets challenge with fear, seeking to understand with questions, seeking answers with anger, desiring peace. You may see in another a mirrored image of yourself.

When you meet friends or strangers who mirror your own self, often you are shaken. They may reflect thoughts or feelings you wish to let go, or do not yet understood. This becomes the lesson, when you come to these challenging situations.

Repeat

**I AM IN THE REALITY OF EARTH
AND SPIRIT AS ONE.
I AM WITHOUT ILLUSION.**

Say:

**I AM IN THE REALITY OF EARTH
AND SPIRIT AS ONE.**

These are difficult keys and the coding of consciousness and most difficult to integrate. You cannot conceive it through the intellect or thought; it becomes part of you through your unfoldment. Each of the keys, are coded for times of future change.

If God is One and One is God and God is many and many are One, where are you and who are you? You are many faces in the many stages of life, living expressions. Say:

I AM WITHOUT ILLUSION.
I AM IN THE REALITY OF EARTH
AND SPIRIT AS ONE.

You will feel the flames of this Light flowing through each and all parts of yourself, continuing in a healing effect.

Accept now the fullness of what you are, the abundance of what you are and the strength of who you are. When awaken ask to see what you must know, know what you must see and accept without question.

Message #2

Love, Light, Spirit and Mind are all aspects of the creation, Creator process. Those whose beliefs do not include, the Creator, have need to understand in symbols as a part of their own spiritual practice. Symbols are universal language presented to those who cannot interpret the consciousness of One Idea, One God, One Principle or One Creator. Buddhism creates symbols for the journey. It is a path with gentle motion. It is a path with tranquility received through the dedication of one's intent to find the essence of compassion within. In the work of Light, you are bridging cultural differences. You are bridging the teachings of Christ through Jesus along with the Wisdom of Buddha and the Laws taught in Hebrew studies. Each code represents a spiritual path related to a different culture. Each one receives insight individually. To integrate the keys and codes is individual.

The Eye: Egyptian

The Crown: Christian

The Spiral: Cosmic/Universal

The Star of David: Jewish

The Lotus: Buddhist

The Cross, Heart & Rose: Christian

The Faces: Native American

The Interlocking Triangles: Esoteric

The Dove: Universal/Christian

The Cornucopia: Native African

The Ankh: Egyptian

As you focus on the Codes and Keys, visualize the energy of the code healing the cultural and national differences healing. From the East to the West and all nations represented, changes are transpiring.

But, in the world as it is seen, in this new millennium, as we have observed, changes have occurred on all levels. Therefore, the bridges of the past are being burned. The conditions, which separated people, are put on the negotiating table to be reviewed and understood through meditative, contemplative, and a spiritual pursuit with healing of Light.

The Key and Code for this lesson relates to perspective. You are, perceiving many perspectives with the help of, "A Course in Light." The Key and Code of Consciousness shows the faces of many, the perspectives of how people see life from their perspective. The faces presented, face both The East and The

West. They are mirrored reflections of both the positive and negative. They are the yin and the yang of consciousness. The Code is the symbol and encodes your consciousness to reflect the deeper meaning.

The key is perspective and the mantra is:

**I AM IN THE REALITY OF EARTH
AND SPIRIT AS ONE.
I AM WITHOUT ILLUSION.**

Everyone sees in accordance to his or her belief. Often belief is in accordance another's perspective, another's experience, another's journey, another's inspiration. In this millennium, each and all will begin to receive a consciousness of unity. It is where you see perceptively there is but One Consciousness linking all, as though there is a unity from one to another, through all the diverse divisions, through all the unspoken perspectives. The thread and the unity is the consciousness understood as the Cosmic Sense. One does not enter into a Cosmic Sense until one has met the conditions of release and healing of the human limitation.

In this meditation, magnify The Key and Code of Consciousness. The Code is the many faces, one to the east and one to the west. Each and all as a symbol of being alike, all mirrored images of another and the Code connects, to the chakra center of the Orange Ray. The frequency of Orange is the lesson of opening to new ways to see, to understand, to bridge the differences and unified all into one.

Say:

WE ARE ALL ONE.
WE ARE ALL MANY OF THE ONE.
WE ARE ALL ONE CONSCIOUSNESS
FROM THE GREATER MIND OF ALL THAT IS.

The chakra center in the frequency of Orange relates to that part of you which is receptive, transmitted by thought, emotion and conditions. It is from this center your physical body is relating to the incidents surrounding you. It is from this center you receive insights and language from others.

In this meditation the Key and Code of perspective is integrated. It links the Light in you and enhances the consciousness within you. The vibration of this ray moves through you to allow you to receive what is being said and how to understand without language of words.

Meditate in this way:

Perceive, you center in a meditative state and your body becomes a transparent Vehicle of Light. You will sense or see, the body is without substance or matter and is energy. Sense you are alive in this Vehicle of Light. You become unlimited by physical matter. Hear, see and know what you are experiencing.

From the masters ...

Many ages ago, we sat in circles and temples, practicing being of No Mind, being of No Body, just being energy. As this came into effect, we were able to be anywhere at any moment. Those abilities shut off as you became denser in your growth. So now remember as though you were in the circle, see the place, know it is you and accept you are integrating that past to the present.

See yourself as the Buddhist Monk knowing you were also a Hebrew Priest, change places, and change faces finding your oneness.

Do you not see how devotion and meditation are of the same experience? Do you not see you can be each one? Each life, whether as a Monk or Priest brings tranquility, peace and compassion? Can you see you, absolutely are attuned to your Divine Guidance in this state of Mind? This is the bridge of perspective and the beginning of Wisdom. From the image as a Hebrew Priest, see your self in the now. Today you are neither monk or priest but fully given the Light. You can perceive you are in holiness. You are in compassion as you were and you now are integrating these aspects.

In the now, feel the Light flow through the solar plexus in you, radiating the frequency, a glow, in the Orange Ray. … See the healing needed for those who are apart of your journey. …

So place in the center of the circle, those who are of your concern, … though you whisper the names and think of them in your mind, your thought draws them to the circle and the Light is released for all of them. …

Speak:

WE ARE ALL ONE.
WE ARE ALL MANY OF THE ONE.
WE ARE ALL ONE CONSCIOUSNESS
FROM THE GREATER MIND OF ALL THAT IS.

Know you are integrating this key.

Be in peace, my beloved ones and may the council ever be the center of your love, the center of your heart, but the wisdom of its consciousness be for all to receive. Go in peace.

When you are ready, you will sense and know you are coming back to the body. Ground your consciousness; anchor your feet, so you can walk sturdily, so it is.

Lesson Eight

COLOR RAY: PINK

The Light of Balance and Perfection

Activate the meditation procedure

Message & Meditation #1

We greet you in the name of the Father, the Son and of the Holy Spirit. Be at peace.

Move with thought into the awareness of your own inner being and rise into the centers of light within the soul plane, activating each frequency to uplift and manifest the vibrations through every dimension of self.

Affirm your completeness and openness to rise into yet other levels of expression.

Bring your awareness into the vibration of the Radiant Pink Ray, the frequency to harmonize, balance and bring all aspects into their highest order. Divine love, manifested through this vibration, helps restore situations in an orderly manner. It is important to release the fear of change within your processes of mental thought. It is important to release fears of projections or how others perceive you. As your faith is strong in truth, in higher wisdom and in the consciousness of divine love, you feel centered.

The fears of human consciousness come into play when they are opposing cosmic sense. The fears of broken structures, the fears of loss of self-identity, all of this creates resistance and brings forth warring factors. As you perceive the outer world, you see a division between beliefs and ideologies. For the earth to become unified will take much time. Ages will come when this particular historical experience will be reviewed as a significant turning point in the evolution of the planet.

The time has come to take a stand and you are called to use your inner strength, inner conviction, truth and know beyond a shadow of doubt, you are a spiritualized consciousness functioning in right action with a greater plan for the destiny of human consciousness.

A cosmic being is an entity of light in direct order with masters of earth conditions and human systems. See its own vibration as a creative source allowing each spirit to express according to its own design. Think on these things.

Look not into your brothers' eyes, without first seeing the potential of the spirit. This is difficult when; one is masked and cloaked in their pain and karmic embattlements.   Each individual is wearing many masks acting out through the individual's journey. However, as one emanates a glimmer of the light through their consciousness, there is recognition on the soul plane. One must accept the brother or sister in light, and with the warmth, love and compassion of their own being. You must not judge another's pathway, but look into the consciousness of their heart.

The message is given, *that to come into focus with the true Christ,* one must come in openness, in faith and in recognition of the minuteness of one's own self, yet overshadowed by the consciousness of the higher expression. Know who you are and claim the consciousness of the Christ as your true overseer, as your true master, as the element that transmutes all imagery.

How difficult it is for this awareness to become fully accepted. The illusions of the earth can stand as a wall to this realization. Yet, until Cosmic Sense is awakened in the masses, it cannot be actualized.   Therefore, many will fear or deny the possibility. Allow your spirit and strength to move through you and you will be empowered in light, empowered in love and empowered in divine consciousness.

All of you are as independent spirits working towards this consciousness. Each of you are moving towards a point where you will be able to perceive yourself in clarity of mind, body and spirit. Do not be disheartened or disillusioned, you are strong as long as you maintain your inner strength and your sense of higher goals. As long as you perceive yourself in right action with the nature of love, the principles of spirit, you will become strong leaders helping others. Let love be the course of your consciousness.

As the Radiant Pink Light moves throughout your nature, experience the clearing and cleansing of all that appears to be in disarray. Come into the higher phases of your own expression within the temple. Release all emotions and perceptions manifested as disillusionment, pain and negativity. Release the burden and heaviness within emotional consciousness, see your heart open and free to explore every avenue of love. Perceive healing coming into focus within individual bodies to bring alignment into circulatory, organic and cellular consciousness. Once more, feel the healing vibration of this Pink Ray as it aligns the bodies and heals disruptions that occur between different levels of awareness.

Know the light and all you have is functioning with ease, with power and right balance. Call upon the Christ within your own expression.

There will be those outside the lessons of *A Course in Light* who will see and recognize what is happening with you. When this occurs, there will be joy and openness, a surprise of the impact the light created. Walk with the light and walk with joy, affirming you are all of what you intended to bring into motion. Go in peace.

Key & Code 8

Interlocking Triangles

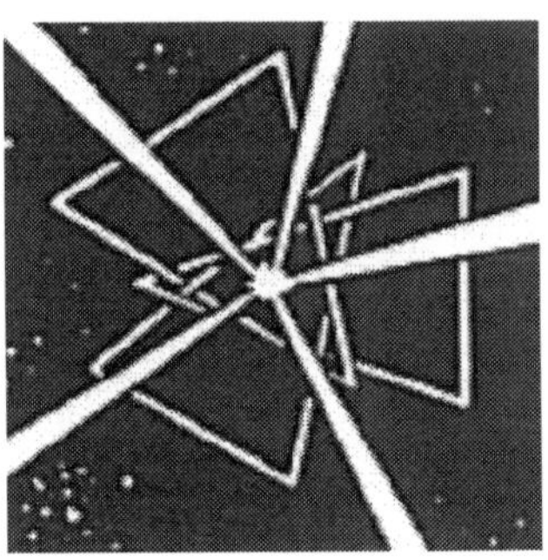

The Code is Interlocking Triangles

Triangles represent a form of balance. Light forces that are triangular or combined light forces represent balance in the universe.

The Key is the mantra:

**THE DIVINE LIGHT OF CREATION
AND CREATOR
UNITES WITH THE PERFECTION
OF THE SPIRIT IN MAN
AND MAN IN SPIRIT TO ITS UNIVERSAL SELF.**

In the frequency of this Light, feel as though conflicts of your ego give way to the energy of a higher vibration drawing you to inner beauty and Light. Coming to these plateaus of peace draws you onward in your quest for higher intent. In moments of bliss, feel a connection to the god-self and what guides you on your path to self-realization.

The keys for this particular lesson are many and yet one. Imaging keys or codes can complicate the concept. Yet, images are how you understand the language of light. This language is readable at any point in time or at any place in time. Therefore, the key represents the idea of love, perfection and balance. It represents the divine love of the god-self and earth-love of the physical-self.

The Code as an image is the key, which unites the idea of the unattainable, attained and earthliness lifted to a heavenly expression.

The Code is the interlocking triangles. Triangles always represent balance. An idea that is triangular or of a combined Light force represents a balance in the universe. The point of light is the center of the interlocking triangles.

How is love understood through these images? How is love represented by these linear descriptions of thought or ideas?

The image of universal love must represent the idea of God as Creator, creation and divine law in its absolute. The Code is the interlocking triangles with the point of Light in the center and the symbol representing the language of God, the image of God, the consciousness of creation as God.

The Key is:

**THE DIVINE LIGHT OF CREATION
AND CREATOR
UNITES WITH THE PERFECTION OF SPIRIT IN MAN
AND MAN IN SPIRIT TO ITS UNIVERSAL SELF.**

Meditate on these keys to receive its imprint within you. Messengers come to you from other planets traveling in vehicles unfamiliar to your physical world carrying within them languages of Light. Those who travel in such, come as messengers for the inter-relation of the physical worlds of earth to the higher worlds of Light. They come not as enemies, but as ambassadors of truth.

They are not the only visitors to your planet, but you will sufficiently find their messages coming through many different channels. Hear their truth.

Love what you know as truth and accept it as so. Others who come **without** the divine intent may confuse the ego systems and place detriment in your path. Stand firm with the Christ as your key and code of truth and use the symbols of your consciousness. They cannot hold you prisoner as you stand in your wholeness and love.

Speak your mantra:

**THE DIVINE LIGHT OF CREATION
AND CREATOR
UNITES WITH THE PERFECTION OF SPIRIT IN MAN
AND MAN IN SPIRIT TO ITS UNIVERSAL SELF.**

We have sent this message for reasons and you will discover the necessity of these reasons. This is not to place undue anxiety on you, but to allow you to recognize that you do not walk alone as a human family without others in your midst.

Beloved ones see your self as The Eye and with the coded key of the interlocking triangles. Realize the center as a focus point. Let body, mind and soul be in harmony. Opening to the next plateau is the door of your acceleration to self-wholeness.

As I speak, many things are in focus. Ask for bliss, ecstasy and joy. When you return to the body, all will be connected. Go in peace.

Lesson Nine

COLOR RAY: AMETHYST

The Light of the Warrior

Activate the meditation procedure

Messages & Meditation #1

Greetings, this is Azreal. We speak again to the light of your higher selves and the egos of your consciousness. Bring them forth into the Radiant White Light and experience once again the vibration of your own soul's expression. Activate each chakra center to free yourself from any negativity manifested through the past cycle of experience.

Once again, release all concerns of the materialistic levels and release concern of coming effects manifesting through change. All things are moving in the direction for the freeing-up of the movement of light.

You are all in the radiant essence of the Amethyst Ray. Release now the conflicts, psychic attachments and all thoughts, words and deeds causing difficulty and conflict. Perceive the Amethyst Ray of Light clearing disease, disharmony and all negativity within. Perceive the soul body of your individual self in a higher frequency. Perceive the light flowing through the soul body and clearing all factions that would limit its source of service.

Your souls are very radiant and are the source of your true nature. Love every element of your consciousness. Perceive this love envelop the body and clear the body of all negative conditions.

92

Feel the energy of the Radiant Amethyst Ray releasing all conflict against itself, releasing conflict within the body systems.

Perceive the body uplifted and releasing all conditions that deny its beauty, its purity, its sensitivity and its own function. Perceive the body and the soul as one focus, as one vibration, as one expression. Perceive the marriage of soul to body united and bonded by the Christ Consciousness. Perceive that the eminence of the spirit of love moves through every facet of your expression.

Now perceive the soul body of the center of light. To perceive is to experience information through the sensory aspect. Consciously know you are experiencing an expansion. See the soul body as an accumulation of every individual life and all aspects of your consciousness. See the soul body enveloped in the radiance of light, in the energy of the Radiant Amethyst Ray. Love all aspects of yourself and love all individuals of your life. Free each one to explore the adventure of their own unfoldment and feel the protection of the light as it envelops all systems.

You are not alone, for the presence of the guides and teachers work in and through you. As you focus, center and clear, feel the joy and light awakening and creating tremendous intensity for your own expansion. There is work for each one who is willing to accept that action. There is a creative outlet for all, who are willing to understand the nature of their soul's desire. Fulfillment comes to each of you.

The effect of your vibration is beyond what you can understand in the conscious sense, but know to cut through the diversities and the opposing factions with love is most important. Express according to the inner nature and you will find yourselves blessed. And now, go in peace.

Message #2

Joshua

Know many held in states of pain or self-denial will feel the door closed on their consciousness until they are ready to understand the nature of the spiritual sense. The coming of the spiritual sense is imminent as manifested in the earth system. Those who recognize its consciousness are feeling the intensity of creating the proper order for the service and for the work to bring others through their own denial systems. As beacons of light, you each have an important part to play in the work of light, in the work of consciousness, in the spiritual effect of accelerating the growth of all systems.

We perceive confusions are all from a source of fear. All fear is a denial of the higher expression. The fear aspect creates blockages to knowing love will bind one into a higher vibration. Know, *without a shadow of a doubt*, your true nature moves through transformation. You each know your physical bodies have brought forth tremendous change in every aspect. You are still processing the old form and creating the new form. As you become integrated and fully expressed, you find the strength of your inner self more dominant than past conditioning. The strength comes from knowing Divine Guidance is the effect of your everyday experience. Therefore, put aside all thoughts of being without connection to your inner nature. Put aside the fear of losing control of your life, for through this release you will find a greater reward than what you can perceive on a conscious plane.

At this particular point in your evolution, you will find the vibrations will be intensified more as you release fear of what you say, how you act and how you are functioning on the personality level.

Again, the quantum leap is manifesting very intently through all who are willing to see, know, experience and accept guidance as the true activity. Many are called to open their eyes and see the greater vision. Think on these things.

Many are lost in the veil of the intellect, so to speak. As the intellect dissipates the spirit, they are proceeding to create a mental disorder within themselves. It is important to see the light in those who feel bondage and pain. See those you love and know, all in the Radiant Warrior Ray. As you become more adept in using the energy and light, you protect your own energy from dissipation. Stay centered on the higher truth and you will overcome the conflicts around you. Do not let the warring or the conflicts dissipate your own inner knowing. Do not allow those who are without resources for the higher wisdom dissipate your own spiritual expression.

We see much joy coming in recognition of light and love overcoming darkness. We perceive many seeking this integration and feeling the intensity of light energy.

You prepare to be receptive to the concept of living *consciously* in many levels of existence. You prepare to see yourself unlimited as a presence of light. You prepare for being both caretakers of things to be cared for, and receptive to the inner strength, connecting you towards opportunities at hand.

The millennium presents to the human race a time of great decision, of manifesting total conscious choice for living as a peaceful species of life in the earth. It is a time of commitment to *laying down of arms* against defenses of illusions of fear, and embracing a totally different structure of personal communications.

There are many different obstacles to this call for human evolution. The oppositions include not only the patterns of the past, but of influences from outside of the earth itself. There is a great concern over maintaining a level of life as it has been and now. In the pattern of historical evolution, the high powers of the earth hold the concept of changing the patterns of relationships to a total new order and citizenship to the universe.

Messages we bring you in small groups are, also received by those governing the activities of humanity. It takes much to accept these patterns of thought, to override the patterns of the fear from the past.

In moments of your meditative state, it is so important you consistently embrace the idea of the earth itself being lifted in its vibrational consciousness and restored order to man, individually, collectively and to the soul of man, and to its own patterns of evolution.

There is much war that cannot be seen, but yet, permeates the energy of consciousness. As you are many as one, perceive the radiance of this light The Amethyst Ray, the great warrior of energy linked to many others who are seeing the earth not at war with other worlds, not at war with other nations, but walking towards an evolution of a different state of life.

So, beloved ones seek to envision the light in all of its many hues manifesting intensely in and throughout all of the planet's consciousness. Perceive that the blindness of man in his illusion has changed to the open eye, to the open ear, to the open heart and to the essence of soul in its highest truth.

Perceive the leadership not crumpled under past fears but strong in direction to resolve, to uplift and to heal. Perceive the empires of the world changing from self-power into global restoration, reformation and healing.

Perceive that man nurtures himself, and fulfills his own abundance through the sharing of its creativity, movements of spirit and light. The physical world is in need of its own attention and manifestations. It is the consciousness that will change the view within the mental and material worlds of life.

Call the great warriors of light, those in spirit and those in body to come to Council and open the ear to hear the eye to see and to acknowledge the power beyond itself to come to truth and peace.

Perceive those who would deviate man from his evolution shielded against the vibrations of this order of the earth's experience. Perceive those who would deny the human spirit connecting to the law and fulfilling the law itself. Send your thoughts that the earth rebuilds, replenishes, restores, reforms, recreates, redirects and flows in harmony.

Perceive all the technology recognized for its greater opportunity to balance human evolution. Perceive the air of the earth and the waters of the earth be replenished with purity and light. Perceive a great calling of the families of the earth connecting and linking to change without fear. There can be no ending to the meditative experience, there can only be moments in which you change from one level to another.

When you are ready to return, focus on your physical self and ground to the physical. Know you come back and settle into your body wakened with a new vision, acceptance and inner peace.

I am Joshua. I have been with you before. Walk with love.

Key & Code 9

THE DOVE

The Code is The Dove

The Dove is the symbol of new beginnings. It is the symbol of a spiritual union between The Creator and Creation. It is also the symbol of peace.

The Key is the mantra:

**FATHER, MOTHER, GOD
CREATOR OF ALL
DESCENDS LIKE A DOVE TO ALL THE EARTH FAMILY
UNITING THE SPIRIT OF ALL THAT IS
TO IT'S SOURCE.**

To those unfamiliar with the symbol, the Dove represents the coming of the Cosmic Consciousness or Christ Consciousness. The descent of the Dove into the human family is a movement from one perspective of experience to a broader perspective of all that is. The Dove is the vibration of Light in the Keys and Codes of consciousness for individuals and groups associated with certain vortexes within the physical plane.

Message

We speak for the council concerning the messages needed for the earth development.   Much has transpired through the coming together of those who assist in the evolving life path of the families of the earth and those of other planes. All the messages have been concerning the time in space in which the descent of the Dove is in motion.

The coming of the dove is in preparation through many generations. You are all a part of this activity. You, as receivers of these Keys and Codes of Consciousness, are peacemakers.

It is important for each and all to hear the message as presented. The keys and the codes to the evolution of self appear in many fractions of ideas and thoughts. Each of the codes imparts a certain recognized symbol connecting you to your station from which you emerged.   A station can be as mansions in many worlds and universes beyond.

Even as we present you with a key or a code, it is a part of many. You may receive or respond to certain codes differently, but the presentation of this work is to enhance the development of your frequency systems as in body, mind, soul to spirit, to raise the vibrational rate of each and all inner planes taking you beyond to inner levels and stations of thought.

The Christ, The Lord of all the physical worlds known to you, gave to each and all the keys to the other worlds. The keys hidden in stories and presented as lessons are found in the Holy Bible. These stories and lessons open hearts and plant the seeds of things to come.

The human soul and the human self is in a stage of change. Some more openly are adapting to the heightened state of Light, others are plodding through resistance, denseness and fear. But, as you have entered into this particular way for inner growth, you are receiving keys and codes to change the molecular structure of your body, the origination of the codes relating to the physical family of your earth. This may cause you to feel not only more unified with all that is, but you will truly understand the deepest meaning of this consciousness.

Your families are not your enemies; they are your connections to the earth, to the lessons of your journeys of many life experiences and are your opportunities for developing understanding, wisdom, freedom and love.

Though resistances and separations still exist in relations, let go of the thought you are an enemy, unaccepted, misunderstood or misplaced. Accept your role within the totality of your family unit. You may be the key that brings them through their spiral of Light to their higher point of consciousness.

As I speak, we ask you to image yourself now as the Dove. The symbol of The Peaceful Warrior is the Dove of Peace. This is a dichotomy for a warrior in your thoughts, is one who goes to battle with weapons and tools to destroy. The true warrior is symbolized as the Dove, the descending Dove of Peace. When the Dove descends into consciousness, so the battle is over, it has been won. When the Dove is fully realized within, it has claimed its victory over all conflicts. The Dove is always the symbol of new beginnings, of a spiritual union between The Creator and Creation, between the sons of Light, The Father of All That Is and the human journey.

Say:

**FATHER, MOTHER, GOD
CREATOR OF ALL
DESCENDS LIKE A DOVE TO ALL THE EARTH FAMILY
UNITING THE SPIRIT OF ALL THAT IS
TO IT'S SOURCE.**

You are in an energy pattern. You have tribes of human lives who have the symbols of birds to represent their spirits soaring, such as, the eagle eye, the hawk, the owl and the raven. All these are symbols of spirit within, now you are The Doves.

We ask you to image the Dove, not only for yourself as an individual expression, but see it as a descent of consciousness touching the spirit of all life. From that spirit, see humanity receiving the image of The Divine Plan for earth's movement through change. The descent of the Dove is also the symbol of Cosmic Consciousness relating to the monadic self.

Now as I speak, see all the symbols you have received. Allow yourself to hear, feel the alignment of these symbols to your consciousness.

The Key is the mantra:

**FATHER, MOTHER, GOD
CREATOR OF ALL THAT IS
DESCENDS LIKE A DOVE
TO ALL THE EARTH FAMILY
UNITING THE SPIRIT OF ALL THAT IS
TO ITS SOURCE.**

You can be one like the Dove, soaring through earth's own fields of Light, bringing the message of peace.

Lesson Ten

COLOR RAY: MINT GREEN

The Light of Renewal and Rejuvenation

Activate the meditation procedure

Message & Meditation #1

We continue in our series of presenting you with the mastery of life. Mastery of life is becoming aware of choices connected to the Law of One. Mastery of life is not denying self through deception, grief or separation from love. The mastery of life is recognizing divine law is the governing thread connecting all of life, regardless of what manner it chooses to express.

Mastery of life is finding that part physically, impassioned to express.   Mastery of life is attaining a status of acceptability to fulfill impulses, joy and ecstasy. A master faces fear to overcome its threat of disharmony. A master of life is one who finds keys to live in harmony, has disciplined the mind, an open heart and a loving inner and outer manner.

We speak to you on the mastery of life for this particular reason. Many are descending into the earth who have achieved mastery and who are open to the possibility of being seen, heard and recognized again.   The difficulty of the mastery of lives in previous times is the same illusion and the fears prevalent in the present earth experience.

It is difficult to master oneself with distractions in so many areas of life in the present earth experience. You can recognize the masters coming through children newly born, by their purity and innocence. Their eyes seem to drink in all of life and speak back to you things unspoken. Your children and your children's children will bring more masters back to the planet.

We do not see an ending of human existence within the planet. There are criterias important in times ahead. You have already moved through certain criteria energy points within the planet. It has been times of inner decision and inner acceptance of one's own self in spiritual growth. It has also been a decision for humanity as a whole to change the patterns of life to a different priority and focus. These are in effect.

What you have witnessed in changes of ideologies and practices of social systems of life, demonstrate the commitment at deep levels to make choices allowing freedom. There are good choices that have come into effect in recent times. There are also resistances to higher consciousness and warring choices made. You cannot control choices or leaders denying, life and holding their subjects in fear of death. Beloved ones do not look to your life as ending, but as a beginning step to other adventures in which you will fulfill strong connections of your soul.

The mastery of life is more than an idea; it is becoming a clear Mind, Body and Soul. Your clarity cannot come when you have confused life with priorities that deny you the ability to live. Think on these things.

We see concerns within each of you, regarding important matters of your daily energies. Trust. The time has come when the choices you make inwardly will demonstrate the Will of your inner self. You may find you are blocked from fulfilling certain ideas or thoughts. This too is a guidance governing your life choices. Trust the inner actions now in effect. Trust in the process that brings you to your freedom. Note there is guidance surrounding you. Let your love and who you are be expressed in fullness.

Key and Code 10

The Cornucopia

The Code

The Cornucopia and the horn have a similar form. A horn represents the sound of announcing a new beginning, a new birth, change and manifestation. The Cornucopia represents what develops from seeds of the mind, the heart and the body and includes planet Earth. It represents the harvest of the Mind, Body and Soul.

The Key is:

**FATHER, MOTHER, CREATOR OF ALL
BRINGS TO EARTH
THE FULLNESS OF ALL
THE MANY WORLDS.**

All initiates come to the Light to receive the keys and the codes to your new self. We are going to present this lesson as a memory, a memory of incidents you have all participated in.

Ceremony and Celebration:

For group study have each student bring some food to create a table of celebration.   A feast all can enjoy for this beautiful ceremony of the Cornucopia.

Prepare a table with a Cornucopia filled with fruit, grapes and breads.   Place Silver or Golden Horns on the table. Place a beautiful Mint Green tablecloth for accent.   Have a goblet for drink.

This presentation to you is a ceremony. It is a ceremony of new life and new beginnings.   It represents manifesting the harvest of life.

The key and the code for ceremony is **The Cornucopia** filled with the harvest of food, such as the fruit of life.   There is also the symbol of **The Horn**.

The Cornucopia and the horn have a similar form.   A horn represents the sound of announcing a new beginning, a new birth, change and manifestation.   The Cornucopia represents what develops from seeds of the mind, the heart, the body and includes planet Earth. It represents the harvest of the Mind, Body and Soul.

The key is:

**FATHER, MOTHER, CREATOR OF ALL
BRINGS TO EARTH
THE FULLNESS OF ALL
THE MANY WORLDS.**

Affirmation:

I AM FULLFILLED.
I AM IN COMPLETION WITH MY SOUL.
I AM EXPRESSING ALL MY GIFTS

The fulfillment of this affirmation comes when the emptiness is recognized. You feel the emptiness before you can be fulfilled. You come to the place in your thoughts, words or deeds as the ending (completion) before you open to receive your bounty.

If your hands feel empty or your heart feels cold, if your feet feel shaky as if you stand on sand and the world seems dark without Light, you are in the state of release. It is a blessing in disguise. It is a step along the way. Let the emptiness, the cold, the darkness and the void be accepted and understood. Confront your fear; this too is illusion.

You must fight yourself. Strengthen yourself to move through the darkness, through the void, through the fear, the emptiness, the trembling and the loss. Awaiting you is the symbol of bounty of harvest, of fruitfulness of celebration and abundance.

Meditate on the key of fruitfulness, abundance and life, the Cornucopia.

Complete this ceremony and bring to the table a gift to share with each other. Bring a symbol of your life and yourself as a living experience of love. You are to create the ceremony, the banquet and passionately enjoy this time, for you are blessed.

Standing with you at this ceremony are those who have helped to assist you in your spiritual path. See, you received these experiences very quickly; the process of understanding it will be with you over a long term of growth. Excited in your internal and external development, you are all ready for your next stage. Let the openness of the heart receive the gifts.

Message

Yes, this Annanius, and I am once again touching the thoughts in you and helping you to see past the illusions of this challenge which stands before you and lifts you to a place where the vision you are seeing, is a vision of a new beginning for all humanity's consciousness. All the events you have seen are part of a beginning to new developments for the human experience of living.

Unifying humanity must come by perceiving the differences as unique and acceptable, and seeing the sameness as the link that connects all as one. In the challenge that is now before you, you are seeing the division of consciousness based upon the schools of thinking, where evil is the side of the experience that is always the opposite point of view. Looking at evil from a perspective where it is outside of yourself but reflected to you becomes quite uncomfortable. In order for this thought of evil to be resolved, there must be a perspective of love within, seeing it as a reflection of the very Light of love in you.

Change is in effect, and in order for all to be apart of the new stages, there are important shifts that must occur. You are those drawn into new energy bodies of your own. You are being lead to go within your own consciousness. From this perspective, you begin to see you are entering a new stage of your evolving self and it is good.

The Keys and Codes are vibrations that assist you, as you assist others in awakened too. Each key represents a small phase of the language of your soul. Words are not adequate, so symbols are given. The symbols become just an imprint of an idea that connects you to the language of the Light within you. So, the key that is most effective in this moment in time is the key associated with the abundance of life and it comes to you as a horn of plenty. As a key, it relates to a banquet of thanksgiving. It can be a symbol of all the abundance of life, collected within a horn of plenty or a cornucopia.

This symbol is a relative idea that abundance is an absolute and always a key within you. Abundance must be understood not in the form of coins or money, but as an aspect of life, that is full, rich and the total source of your Creator's Consciousness. Abundance must be seen, as an absence of lack. Abundance must be understood, as a principle by which you live. There should be no thoughts of lack, based from fear "that nothing good will be and darkness will occur." Abundance is seen, as the absolute state in which "everything required is right there."

Focus now on this frequency, The Code. Words cannot describe, yet it is a sound, it is a light, it is a pattern and it is a consciousness.

The key is:

**FATHER, MOTHER, CREATOR OF ALL
BRINGS TO EARTH
THE FULLNESS OF ALL
THE MANY WORLDS.**

When you are first in creation, you know nothing of separation. When you first are born from The Source, your creation knew nothing of emptiness, only fullness. When you descended in the dimensions of the earth, you began to sense and see there was a lack of your continuity. You began to fall into patterns of separation; you begin to lose what you knew to be the total reality of oneness.

The Horn of Plenty or the Cornucopia is the symbol of **abundance** as in the beginning of your consciousness awakening to your true identity.

The mantra is:

**FATHER, MOTHER, CREATOR OF ALL
BRINGS TO EARTH
THE FULLNESS OF ALL
THE MANY WORLDS.**

Affirm: All that I need and all that is, are within. All that is within is, abundantly connected to what I know and what I think.

This is a Principle and Key to knowledge. To know, to see, to accept and be is what leads you to higher reality.

Accept the keys imprinted within you. Release to the light whatever doubts have been a part of you. All you see as lack and emptiness is a form of separations from the consciousness of your source.   See, know and let it be, God is all and all is He and She.

From this key, allow your consciousness to expand connecting to all others raised in consciousness like you. Perceive you are one with all the family of humanity.   Even though there are differences, perceive abundance in the very core of their essence. Truly, the key of peace, which you all seek so intensely, is the key of fullness, abundance and wellness in its spiritual perspective.

How do you experience this key, share it and relate with it? First, meditation must be for releasing any opposition to accepting your great abundance.   Look at your thoughts regarding lack and limitation. Look at your thoughts of separateness and focus on the higher truth. Let the Light come through and raise that part of you. To share the abundance is to give freely without expectation.

From this place and center of light, trust and know what appears to be devastation surrounding you and all the things that are apart of this, healed from the illusion.   There is no lack, only change. There is no destruction, only clearing. What appears to be the war

109

of the ages is the war eternally, individually and collectively. So heal the war in you and let the peace come through, stand upon your higher truth knowing abundance is the absolute.

Share this with all and let it be, "there is no fear in humanity." The abundance of life can be felt individually. Those who take away from another are blocking the highest consciousness that comes from the Creator. Observe and stand firm on the truth "that you understand the truth of fulfillment of the earth's new stage of spirituality."

Often spoken in the earlier stages, the keys will not be a process for you. The Keys lead you to acceptance inside and raises everything as a part of you. Each key is to be experienced because of all the former intensities. Accept the keys as being apart of the spiritual path leads you through and into the higher stages of your own full life activity.

We, of The Council, see the struggles so intensely within you, we wish you to know these messages of Light will be apart of what moves the earth and humanity too its own next phase.

So, though the struggles with the challenges seem greater than you wish to bear, it is a masterful path that leads to total wholeness of mind, body and spirit. It embraces all humanity from all *walks of life* it embraces all the spiritual realities and unifies it as one. It is the gift to the planet; it is the key of the highest form of spirit and mind.

All that you are and all you do is totally understood as the challenge of you, but bless it, accept it and know it to be the greater gift for all humanity. Go in peace beloved students. Though you are small in groups, yet you are large in the greater view. From this core consciousness of Light, it moves through and touches the multitudes; it is meant to be. So go in peace and may the beginning of this new phase be planted in your soul and lead you through and into the greater whole.

So, it becomes a connection relative to your past, but brings you forward, through and too the future of everything you do. You will go to other places and sharing what you have become touching those in pain, sorrow and lifting others to their joy.

The council touches you, Azreal, Andrew, Jove, Joshua, Marcus and Moundriny and Peter has joined the group and has added some thoughts for all of you. The Christ Spirit overseers and through Jesus brings messages to all. From the Order of Melchizedek, you connect to these beings of light.

So go in peace and may the beginning of this new phase be planted in your soul and lead you through and into the greater whole.

Lesson Eleven

COLOR RAY: SCARLET

The Light of Passion

Activate the meditation procedure

Message & Meditation #1

Marcus

Greetings once again, beloved students of light, we sense you are experiencing a change in your total perspective of who you are. You are extremely desirous to attain Cosmic Consciousness so you can experience total vision, understanding and wisdom

The exercises given through my brother, Azreal, have afforded you the opportunity to work intensely within the soul plane with healing light and the intensity of vibration and elements of the cosmic rays. You are now at the brink of moving into another plane of expression. I, Marcus, will gather other sources of Minds to guide you through the inner centers to free the mental nature from aspects that would deny your true consciousness.

In the silence, focus on the plane of the soul level and rise with your senses into this dimension. See your soul center as a rainbow of consciousness. As you activate each frequency, experience its effect on your body.   Let the bodies be still; let the minds be still; let the thoughts be still. Focus in the clear hues and direct the light to any areas in discontent or in dis-ease.

If you feel pressure within the mind, magnify the rays within this mental plane. The spine is the key to alignment, polarity and physical wholeness. When the spine is off-center, the energy flow through the bodies is not able to clearly complete its own direction. Healing your own body, mind and spirit is a constant process.

Gather together with the ascended masters, teachers and thought adjustors within the Planetary Center. Perceive in this moment the brilliance of this Radiant Scarlet energy. Meditate with this energy, the energy of desire, the passion of your soul and power of light ray. Contemplate your reaction, if given the power to achieve whatever you came to express. If you had the power what would be your experience?

The lessons of this particular frequency are many. The lessons of selfish intentions, manipulation of others for personal wealth, power and greed can be the obstacles for those who are swept up in a false intention. Therefore, think on power.

What is power to you?

If the human mind could return in openness to its true inner place and intent of its first knowing in full empowerment, what would be the outer result?

The last temptation of Jesus Christ involved the testing of His power.[3] This is the great test of all in the spiritual path to enlightenment.

---

[3] Luke 4 1-13 The Holy bible

The order or decree sent to all in the path of enlightenment is to accelerate, increase and magnify the lessons and light. The earth is beginning to move into an accelerated vibration. Therefore, many are experiencing a sense of imbalance as well as changes in perspective of their own conditions.

Activate the cosmic light of the Radiant Scarlet Ray through the networking of energy; see this vibration as the motivator bringing all things to the highest manifestation.

The warring factors are increasing and intensifying within every element of the earth. It is difficult as lightworkers to remove your consciousness from anxieties and intensities of injustice created by inversions of power. Understand the karmic imbalances are brought into rightness.

Nations upon nations are meeting the creations of ancient thought, expression and past desires to current struggles for freedom and power. The enmity between nations is in a state of explosiveness. Perceive the earth enveloped in the cosmic energy to transmute egos swept away in their webs of evil or misuse of power. Affirm all nations open to understand the movement into Universality of Mind.

Affirm the turning away from the destructive consciousness and move toward the consciousness of the Builder and Creator of Peace.

We, of light, move through your being. We become a part of your soul systems to magnify and intensify the cosmic plan for the earth's true evolution. Hold your silence.

In the next cycle of this Spiritual Path to Enlightenment of Planetary 8 intense work takes place for clearing the remnants of repetitive past life karmic activities of the **Soul Causal Body.**

You have all participated in many eventful moments recorded throughout history, both for human evolution and de-evolution, as they existed simultaneously.

For every soul who has broken through the barriers of negativity and walked in the light, there are those who held back and joined forces creating negativity and dissipation of humanity.

I, Marcus, have chosen to work with The Mind, the intellect and the disciplines of thought processes. We work to empower the Mind with consciousness of its own divinity, to awaken the self to life unending.

Messages & Meditation

It is good to speak again. We are going to reflect on thoughts built in the past by masters of life. Masters have come to the earth to demonstrate the power of the love of the Creator and creations. The passion behind each of these endeavors is stimulated by understanding and faith in things far surpassing human capabilities. Those who brought mastery to the physical world channeled the process through the soul. The soul has initiated the vibration in which the physical would respond.

The mastery of life is initiating soul's own intent with love, intensity and acceptable power to explore the unknown. To master life is *not to falter at the impossible.* Mastery is not lying down before the wall of resistance. Mastery is exploring the way past the illusion of resistance.

If you are ready, beloved ones, to initiate your impassioned self to master emotions, your mental subjective self and all conditions of your life, you are all able to attain the state of spiritual master.

The keys to manifestation of desire is through, Manna, the Mind. The Mind is the initiator of ideas, thoughts and vibration.

The key is:

**MIND AS MANNA,
MANNA AS LIGHT,
LIGHT INTO SOUL,
SOUL INTO CONSCIOUSNESS
AND CONSCIOUSNESS INTO PHYSICAL EXPRESSION.**

Thought from the Mind manifesting as substance retrieved by the soul, imaged by the soul, directed by the egos, explored in the physical realm and built upon with all the acceptance, faith, wisdom and truth. These are your stepping-stones, your building blocks to the foundation that express the mastery of life.

Foundation comes through the Mind and actualizes as soul imprinted through the consciousness of ego systems. You are the caretakers of the foundations of light.

Say:

**THE EARTH IS IN NEED OF THE LIGHT.
THE LIGHT IS THE MASS ACT
OF CONSCIOUSNESS IN EFFECT.
PEACE IS DESCENDING LIKE A DOVE INTO THE HUMAN
SOUL.
THE PROCESS IS IN EFFECT.**

The trembling of the body, the uncertainty of thoughts are all the battles of resistance and fear. As you share the wisdom, share your understanding and help those in the darkness of the soul's night, you open them to the opportunity to find the morning light.

I bring this message to you with love, as a gift of grace and with the power of the essence of this ray of light. We are not going to activate the process in the form of pyramids for this procedure. We simply are directing you to accept this act of light now as an integral part of your individual passion to pursue your goals, your dreams and your understandings.

Through this impact, accept and be focused. When you awaken, all spoken, all in motion will respond within you and become a part of you

You are never far from our thoughts. You are never far from our presence. You are always within a thought away from experiencing our love.

Code and Key 11

The Ankh

The Code is the Ankh

The Ankh represents the symbol of the heart and soul of man and woman, united as one being. It is an ancient symbol coming to us from Egypt.

The Key is the Mantra:

**THE COSMIC MOTHER,
THE COSMIC FATHER JOIN AS ONE,
THE PRINCIPLE OF MANIFESTATION
OF PASSION AND DESIRE**

This lesson is The Key 11; the number eleven is associated with mastery, a master number. Eleven is beyond completion it is integration. It is the unity between two polarities. It is the coming together as one whole being, uniting the mental, physical, emotional, sexual and psychic aspects in you to a non-divided state, neither female or male, but fully active in both the feminine and masculine experience.

This Key and Code symbolize the marriage between consciousness as a creative, dynamic active masculine being, and an open receptive, intuitively connected, feminine being. It symbolizes balance between these areas of your self.

Now the Ankh and the Cross interrelate. The cross represents the crossing out of all the karma as your need for growth. The Ankh represents forgiveness and the coming together in oneness.

These experiences with the keys and codes were also a part of the Atlantian civilization when there still were memories of the connection to the origin of their first light as an individualized being. The Atlantians, when first given the experience of being human, had strong connections to their memory of being part of the hierarchical consciousness of angelic experience. From that spiritual part of them, they came to the physical world to bring that divine source to the physical earth. Through the human nature, they were caught in struggles between the male and female powers. Atlantians diminished in their spirituality as they came into the physical. The physical life depleted their awareness of the divine state.

So, as we see in this time period, there was a breaking of law, breaking down of all the conditions first established as a divine way of living. During the time of Agnaton, perceived to be the god of Ra, there were legends about former gods, these represented the guides of their spiritual journey. During Agnaton's reign, many were highly evolved. There was a time when Egypt reigned on the earth as a symbol of true royalty, as a spiritual self and as a consciousness of Light.

Symbols were given to those who had the memory of the priest inside or the memory of the Light within. The Ankh represented the attainment of getting through and over the conditions of being held enslaved by the physical body, by the sexuality and sensuality that caused negativity in their own past and present time frame.

The Ankh symbolized those who had surpassed or overcome these old issues and became connected to the divine self of a higher cause. The Ankh was given as a symbol to those who came together also in marriage, marriage in a common union of male and female experience. Today the lesson of the Ankh is for those who are ready to see this inner consciousness as Divine Light or as the Christ Consciousness, which lifts itself to its higher experience and to ascension of the soul.

The process is a journey and from this journey, you focus on letting go of external distractions.

Say:

THE COSMIC MOTHER,
THE COSMIC FATHER JOIN AS ONE,
THE PRINCIPLE OF MANIFESTATION
OF PASSION AND DESIRE

Think:

I am not my body. The body is just what I experience but who I am and what I am is of a source totally in its own consciousness.

I am the mind and the heart of the soul of who I am meant to express.

I am the inner Divine Light and the spirit of what guides me.

I am masculine in my creation and I am feminine in my creativity.

I am all that is God's experience through me.

I am released of karmic conditions of pain, resentment and fear.

I am unified with my first cause and creation of God's own essence.

As the essence of this Light magnifies, perceive its flow through you, directed to that part linked to the passion of the soul as you. The activation of this passion is magnified. Experience its vibrant energy flowing through and into every aspect of you.

Say:

**THE COSMIC MOTHER,
THE COSMIC FATHER JOIN AS ONE,
THE PRINCIPLE OF MANIFESTATION
OF PASSION AND DESIRE.**

Now the Ankh and the Cross interrelate. Go in peace and may the Light of the Christ be in and through you.

Key & Code 12

The Diamond

The Code is a Diamond

The Code is like a Diamond of energy. It is symbolic of the vibration of crystalline energy. The Diamond represents all the facets of your thoughts, your mind and all aspects of you comprised as One Consciousness.

The Key is:

**I AM ONE WITH ALL THAT IS.
I AM THE CREATIVE CREATOR
IN CONSCIOUS MOTION AS LIGHT
I AM THE BUILDER
AND FOUNDATION OF THOUGHT.**

Every life form, every intelligent aspect of Light holds within it the design of the triad as pyramids.

Many ask, *"What is the purpose of bringing us such keys and codes?   Of what use can they possibly bring to the physical plane?"*

These are the keys, the language of the soul and spirit. They are the direct communication by ways that connect with other forms of life.

Your planet does not stand alone in the universe, but is a beautiful star where souls returns to over and over again to live out desires unfulfilled and to practice in creative endeavors of thought. It is a planet of extraordinary karma and a planet that lives by the law of the physical plane.   It is astutely receptive to any law, man initiates. The earth is the place you can program your own self to live any form of life you choose and have free choice to perform this life in a manner karmically repetitive.

The Keys and Codes of Consciousness help you move from physical awareness to a higher dimension to assist in a unified manner with other systems of life.   Though these symbols are simplistic ideas, nevertheless they transmit frequencies that are uniform and universal in meaning.

So again, the first key is the Eye, the all seeing, all knowing I Am of your own I AM. When you activate The Eye and ask for the wisdom in knowing, vibrations move through you to assist you in registering ideas and concepts.   The key introduced is the foundation of your consciousness in earth. The pyramid structure called the tetrahedron is associated with the Eye. This pyramid energy is your sacred space to contemplate and assimilate your lessons.

Pyramids are constant unending triangulations or triad forms of light creating multifaceted pyramids.   Every life form, every intelligent aspect of Light holds within it the design of the triad known as pyramids of Light. This is the foundation and grounding center of your essence.

The Twelfth Key and Code represents the completion of all the cycles of evolved consciousness. Twelve is the number of completion of the soul's journey through all of its initiations. The twelfth chakra represents the last aspect of your being within the soul system, which is the conduit for both the life force in you and the dimension of your higher self, the envelopment of you into the Crystalline Light.

There were twelve disciples of Jesus Christ. There were twelve tribes of Israel. There are twelve planets for our universe. The number twelve is symbolic of the stages of development and growth, initiation and completion. The twelfth key represents the frequency of Light experienced at the time of full ascension.

Crystallized forms of light are keys and codes that initiate thought into manifesting its purity and being.

Many colors may come as you see these essences rise up before you. The key of consciousness is:

Say:

I AM ONE WITH ALL THAT IS.
I AM THE CTREATIVE CREATOR
IN CONSCIOUS MOTION AS LIGHT.
I AM THE BUILDER
AND FOUNDATION OF THOUGHT.

There is no limit to the forms of these lighted crystals. They grow and multiply. Your ideas are within these crystals of thought. So it is.

Ask that you are discerning of what you are building and planning. Perceive the planet as your earth, responding to the Light. The Crystalline Light is associated also with the Millennium.

Marcus:

Though we speak to you and awaken you to receive the frequencies symbolically, the actual experience of its impact will come at the time of your full ascension. The ascension is not being *lifted up* and placed into a new planet. Ascension is the completion of your process of the physical body being in full unity with all the many dimensions of your true being.

This key will never be fully realized until everything about you is elevated to a state where you are in complete wholeness with each level of your being. That comes through all the challenges you overcome in your path. That comes when all the lessons become apart of a realization of completion. It comes when the karmic wheel of your life transforms to the wheel of Light as in, love *and grace.*

In speaking to each and all, you are activated to a heightened state, but little of what is in effect will remain with you. What you will be a part of, is directing consciousness to prepare itself for these transformed effects. Each key given has been imprinted into your soul's being and activated within the higher self's vibration.

The twelfth key of the Crystalline Ray is not an activated tool, it is the consciousness of the full Christ Awareness achieved when you have brought yourself through all the uncertainties and stand in wellness.

So, as we speak, be it known Councils of Light stand with you. This moment never can be measured by your thoughts. It can only be experienced as a realization, releasing every attachment from the history of your soul, releasing all the conditions that have bore you down with earthly difficulties and where you are clearing in this consciousness of you any effects causing you to doubt yourself, doubt the power of love or to doubt the source of what comes through.

In speaking for you, observe what comes to you as you walk through this transitional bridge. Accept you are walking through a dimension far beyond what you have been through before. The rays of Light in the frequencies of its intensity overshadow you in all the hues you see as the colors of energy. One may stand more intense or become more bright in your eye, one frequency of color may seem to dominate all but each are a part of the whole.

Accept the code is a Diamond of energy. The code is symbolic of the vibration of Crystalline Energy. The diamond represents all the facets of your thoughts, all the facets of your mind and all the aspects of you comprised as one consciousness as you. In this diamond like vibration, perceive you are in a brilliance of energy surrounded by frequencies. From this, everything in you is changing and lifting you to new dimensions. **You cannot activate this for anyone else. This is what you come to in the moment right for you.**

When all you have overcome is behind you, all you have traveled through is no longer effecting you, when all the pain, suffering and conditions developed are no longer within your mind, within your spirit, you are the Crystalline Light. This is the origin of you, the being as you, in the first cause of your creation. Experiencing this key will affect each in a different way, but as we magnify its vibration stay centered in calmness, in peace and in oneness and observe what is taking place.

Truly know beloved ones, when the karmic wheel has stopped its turn, when life's journeys of all the many experiences of you are all part of one life, one mind and one consciousness you are free in total acceptance forgiven of all that was. You then stand in this Crystalline Ray. It is a vehicle of Light, much as the body of Light, the Merkaba. It is the vehicle taking you through all the other levels. It is the vibration, which transmits your thoughts, to higher realms; its what moves you through time, space and into a place that is familiar to your soul's consciousness.

It is within this Light you see everything with clarity, where what you observe in the physical world is so far removed from what you know is the ultimate plan of spirituality. It is in this light you sense and see the greater plan for the earth is all in alignment with its own pattern of higher reality. It is in this place you can see what appears in the illusions of man's making is just a short cycle of changes for the earth. It is in this frequency you see your own life, not insignificant, but a part of a greater plan. Stay in this frequency and within this clarity let the mind in you be fully connected to accept and understand the power you emanate. Trust all you need to fulfill your own cause and effect. Destiny is manifesting right within you, let go of doubts and fears inside of you.

By the Order of Melchizedek, the imprint of the priesthood is placed upon you. The priesthood is for those who bare and care for the consciousness for the earth. You all have been anointed before in schools of learning, in lives before. You have all been connected with tremendous experiences of spirit, but in this moment of time, you are closest to a full initiation that spirit brings when you have transited to the heightened states of Light. So very few initiations are completed in the body but in these experiences of what we give you, your soul and your body become in wellness, wholeness and completeness karmically freed. Go in peace and so it is

Notes
____

SECTION TWO

PLANETARY 8

SOUL CAUSAL BODY

MEDITATIONS

INTRODUCTION

Purpose

The level of Planetary 8 is a process of working within the Soul Causal Body.

The soul-causal system is the active desire that brought you back into this earth experience. There still may be some aspects within this level holding you locked into some unresolved activity.

As you move through this level, you may find you are less attached to things that seemed important to you in previous levels.

This level brings a release from anxiety of restlessness and driven addictions causing over-reaction to petty situations. Those nagging internal feelings driving you to distraction, ease away as you find yourself allowing life to unfold as it is meant to be.

This level brings great healing and love into your life as many struggles of the previous rounds are completed.

In this level, you are preparing for the impact of energy setting into motion the true purpose of your destined path.

Your personal meditations may not necessarily follow a precise technique. The higher self is the director of your communication. Observe and be a co-pilot of this inner self that attunes to your own personal communication.

The Soul Causal Desire Nature

In the following cycle, you will work intensely on the causal desire nature of your own soul's vibration. The soul causal desire is the aspect of the soul, which brought you into incarnation. It is that part of your nature desiring to express, create, develop, learn, evolve, serve and focus on all activity.

However, the causal desire body an aspect of the Mercabah, soul body of light, is held in bondage through karmic activity past incarnations. You are here repeating incidents of past-life consciousness. The goal is to enter a State of Grace where you are free of these karmic patterns. Each of you draws to yourself effects of causal conditions from past life to present time.

MEDITATION PROCEDURE

Meditation now is a comfortable experience in which you perceive yourself energized as you direct thought into the forebrain.

Observe how your consciousness and the coming together of the egos flow easily to the forebrain moving up into the Star Center. Follow through with the activating of each of the centers in the soul body.

As each center is activated once again, move into the level in which you meet the hierarchy. In the silence, experience your connection to these beings of light.

Connect to the network for planetary work and healing.

You will observe the inner work that takes place individually focuses on the Causal Soul Body.

The causal body of the soul holds the records and desires that brought it back into incarnation. Within the depth of this aspect now there is a release of any and all negative consciousness holding the soul in bondage to its karmic connections. Therefore, in the meditation the guides and teachers of the Council of Light activate the inner work .

When you experience the completion of the inner work during the sessions, draw yourself back into the body and ground your consciousness. Always close off your aura and magnetic field by moving the energy in a clockwise motion.

Lesson Twelve

COLOR RAY: WHITE

The Light of Purification

Message & Meditation #1

Meditate

Activate the meditation procedure gathering awareness to the forebrain and moving into the soul body of light.

In the soul plane, perceive the desire nature of the causal self enveloped in the vibrations of Radiant White Light.

Perceive the desire self reaching into its own past …

Know desire creates, motivates and brings things into action. Without desire, one cannot function.

The purpose is not to dissipate desire, but to clear its activity of negative karma out of past-life conditions. To free yourself, perceive you are in the present, you are in an essence of light freeing all desire attached to anxieties or unfinished actions. Affirm the law of balance releases you from all past soul negativity.

It is beautiful and joyous when you know you have released the negative karma and desires no longer a necessity for your life experience.

You are a soul enveloped in the body. The body is the instrument of the personality consciousness and is subject to human laws and conditions. You must function within its laws. To function as a cosmic being, a balance can be reached on the inner plane between

Cosmic Law and Human Law. Eventually there will be the integration on all levels of existence.

Now concentrate purely on your soul's causal desire nature and feel the impact and vibrations of healing in the inner plane. Let the light be the source of releasing fear, imageries and past negative actions.

Perceive your desire and causal self, absorbed in the vibrations of the White Light. See you're self-integrated with Christ Consciousness. To be Christed means to be an emanation of Cosmic Consciousness. It is the awareness of being not only a member of earth activity, but also a true spirit of interplanetary consciousness functioning within the Law of Love and the Law of Grace.

In your physical life, examine your motivation and desire for creating greater good in all action. As you integrate on all levels, seek what you desire to unfold. Then the Law of Attraction brings opportunity to you like a magnet.

Events on the outer plane will be creating many signs of change. As you stay focused, centered with your understanding and love, you will feel the power of the Presence through all outer circumstances.

The spiritual call goes out to all willing to experience the event that will bring about change. Many will receive the awareness of a Presence coming to them to free their thoughts from past conditioning allowing them to see with a new vision.

Release all concerns about who you are, where you are going and how this will all take place. You are all adventurers preparing and creating an environment of light and love for those who are willing to accept the new life vision and activity.

At times, the body may feel and absorb the lower dense energy forms, but within you stand unshakable against the negativity. As this occurs, you become the strength and personification of a higher consciousness.

It is a difficult road, but perceive your soul is releasing from itself all causal factors that would deny its truth, its strength and its purpose to manifest joy and peace within the earth.

Perceive the energy of the White Ray as consciousness, as love, as joy and as freedom. Feel its essence moving through the planes of the lower bodies clearing all past conflicts.

Spirit knows no boundaries. It lives without structures. It moves and has its being as a free expression. The activity now exemplified, is the individual soul unfolding and fulfilling its highest design. Within the factors of personality consciousness, the masters work with you, not to transport you into other systems, but to uplift, heal and bring alignment into all systems.

This consciousness will present the higher wisdom. The imageries of truth present the messages as given forth from ancient times to present experience. Every round is another journey through activity, experience, adventure and joy.

A Discussion on the Influx of Planetary Energies

As we greet you once again, perceive each of you merged in a plane of activity reaching out into other dimensions. The intellect cannot fully comprehend the actuality of these journeys. Experience the energy of the Radiant White Light moving into the mental body, releasing any thoughts, stresses or anxieties and purifying all sense of negativity. We merge with your being to uplift any factions that lie as a source of discontent within your nature.

Perceive your awareness rising through the center column of light in the radiant vibrant energy of the Christ light. Perceive that the image or experience of this Christ becomes a reality to you in a conscious way. Think not that you are without worthiness to express this indwelling Christ. Know that this indwelling Christ overshadows all that you are and that as your human self is walking in this pathway of life experience, the totality of your consciousness is an exemplified action of the Christ, the spirit that merges all things into their complete wholeness.

The Christ spirit manifested through the life of Jesus is that which unites all souls in its evolving process to become fully and completely one with the Father Godhead. Therefore, think of self as moving through time and life experience with an entirely new perspective, not simply limited to an earthly condition that holds you in states of separation, but as true light bearers of the Christed spirit.

Perceive you are rising up through the frequency rays of energy into the level in which your vibration is free from the form of matter and where you enter a plateau and dimension unified with the Council of Light.

You are the pioneers and teachers of this understanding within the earth plane. For each one as you share the work of light, you become as an Elder Light worker directing others through the mazes of their experience. As they trust your caring, you also trust the care of your family of light workers and those of the hierarchy.

We wish to speak on the events to come in this particular cycle stemming from the influx of planetary energies into the human mind and soul. These planetary energies are to stimulate a regenerative activity and movement towards an evolving consciousness to implant the seed of Spirit with a greater awakening.

It is most important in your daily lives you do not dwell on what appears as the destructive forces of human conditioning, but think more about the energy of light bringing peace into the hearts and minds of the human race. This is not a fantasy, for there will be a time when humanity walks as light, spirit and soul completed in leadership of earth activity.

In the present, the forces that deny the spiritual nature are battling with the human condition. The stresses and strife of materialization have run rampant. The control of creation is out-of-hand; change is in order. Look on this situations dissipated and transmuted into good energy for new creative means.

Nuclear systems utilized in a favorable activity can greatly assist humanity, but too often, its power is held as weapons against the greater good. It is important to once again focus on this part of human's creation and see it brought out the hands of resistance, fear, control and misuse of power. Instead, visualize nuclear energy in the hands of reason and spiritual understanding.

Focus on areas of discontent within the planet. Perceive the energy of light as it touches the inner hearts and mental processes of the human system transmuting and raising the heavier vibrations.

As you see starvation, hunger and death of many people also see The Radiant White Light surrounding the episodes. Though the karmic wheel brought many into these events, compassion and healing is required for those in need. When the idea of wealth as power, love and worth is changed, then productivity will be in distribution in a more balanced manner.

As Trees of Light[4] bearing the fruits of your own consciousness, each of you reach out and touch others at some level in order to bring the activity of peace into its fullness.

---

[4] Planetary Two Initiation Ceremony

Pyramid Light Work

You can activate a pyramid according to your own insight. This is the sacred space of your own energy field. The pyramid is the place you create and form for the healing of your friends, family and all needs.

In this center of love and light no one can disrupt your energy. Let the essence of light be the source of all healing. There is no time limit to meditation. When you have completed your personal time, ground your energy.

Message & Meditation #2 – Master Andrew

You are very blessed among all responding to the changes of the human ego, which is cosmically aware of its own place within the nature of life in spirit. You are blessed.

The soul itself loves to live, move and have its being among the experiences that reflect its own image of life. The soul you have so awakened too has played in all the many journeys of life. The human aspect brought the soul to many experiences that have caused it to find the necessity to return to cycles within the earth.

The soul may hold regret or excitement. The soul may hold all the impressions that the human heart knows. From this particular reality in spirit, we demonstrate to you a consciousness of healing to alleviate within the depth of the soul, repetitious patterns that cause it to feel uncertain, destroyed or in shadows of pain. So, be patient as the work is transpiring through you. Again, we cannot take away the lessons needed for understanding, depth, wisdom and spiritual evolution.

Much of the impressed conditions are released through your own surrender to the will of higher guidance and light. The alleviation of disorder, disorientation, confusion, restlessness and pain occurs in the light.

Many would hold this in a doubtful place in mind, having no sense of relation to a soul impression.   Whether it is in body or out of body the soul knows its self to be alive, able to think, able to move, explore and connect to consciousness of creativity.

In the vibrations of this energy which clears, purifies and releases, experience now the impact of these radiant particles of light upon you, within you and within the soul body.

As the breath of life is breathed into consciousness, feel you are also letting go of deep concerns and fears of guilt over patterns repeated and karmic negativity within the soul,.

Affirm the negative repetitions of patterns released to the light.

Affirm the remaining aspect of desire be what stimulates the soul to its greater strength, purpose and light to heal.

Ceremonies of many of schools take the initiate to the place of purification.   White Eagle perceives how the great circles of Native Americans created ceremonies for purifying the body and the mind from conditions that cloud its vision. The meditations and visions instill the flow of thought and vision from the ancient ones to the present time.   Many ceremonies give help to initiate the soul through its karmic phases into release from impurities.

To many the ceremonies of purification require water to drink or a bath. If flowing water comes to your own imagery, feel yourself in a pool of water.   Water is an aspect of your life and planet Earth. Water is a necessity to maintain balance and centering. You gravitate to water to be refreshed, rejuvenated, released, cleared and severed from stress and pain.

The vision for all is the vision of perceiving the waters of the earth restored to its clear perspective, to envision the deep, deep concerns that the pollutants have brought into effect, and to see these difficulties of karmic entanglements being cleared by reason.

The process of this particular energy will be with you. There is no time limit to the particular experience. Recognize you are in an experience of in depth inner healing. …

When you are complete with this meditation, direct your ego systems to return to the physical.   In the return to the bodies, accept clearing, stability, strength and joyful movement in accepting growth. Go in peace.

Message: White Eagle

Peace, I bring to you and my Presence surrounds you.

You are all brothers and sisters. You are all seekers on a path for peace. This is White Eagle and I come with honor. To bring honor to you is to fill you with the worthiness to receive the symbol of peace. To achieve the honor to receive this, empty yourself of your doubt. Together you council with those who guard your spirit and there are many.

You each have connections to times you have lived before and lives you have lived in simple ways, much as the Native Americans in their early years of earth. In the earliest times, there no was separation between the body and the spirit and the memory of the Light. But as the body became denser from the broken law, the broken arrow, the broken treaties, the broken trust, the wall of separation occurred. It was only through those who still had sight, the Shaman, the Chief who would be in connection with the ancient ones who walked before them.

The nation I directed was a nation of incarnated souls that lived with great happiness in the heart and satisfaction with their simplistic lives. But, all was disrupted when change came into effect and the nation became broken until the Trail of Tears was in effect. But the Order of Melcizedek and Lord Michael and Christ lifted the shadow of a darker state and connected too the consciousness of being Chief of all that experience. And now I speak with you to help bridge in the heart of you and in the mind of you, history of your past.

The lesson is acceptance of peace.

In the past, you would spend many days preparing for such a sacred moment. But in dimensions of Light and the essence of soul, time is of no matter. And through the path you walk with Light Work, you are clearing and cleansing much of yourself.

So now: **White Eagle sang the healing tones**.

…

Peace cannot come until you have become peace within the heart of you. The healing of your consciousness is such and it is good.

White Eagle sings a second healing song of tones, different than first.

…

Vibrations of those sounds will clear your mind and now receive the essence of peace. Whatever the fear created in your life, it is no longer the power it was. Yes, you must walk through the challenge before you guided along the way, every day.

…

Now hold the pipe of peace in front of you and sense from it you are receiving the vibration to transmit a Light throughout all that surrounds you, all that you are connected with throughout the earth in need of peace. War and battles become the conflict of a heart.

There is nothing so difficult that you cannot overcome, but you must see with the eye of the eagle. You must become like an eagle above what you see in the illusion of earth. To have the eye of the eagle is to have the connection of the Great I Am.

...

Accept you can see and accept that you can be all that is meant for you.   And now be path walkers, light on your feet, strong in your mind, clear in your eye and wisdom in your heart.

Lesson Thirteen

COLOR RAY: GOLD

The Light of Transmutation

Message & Meditation #1

New Order in the Earth and Planetary Service

In this cycle of the light lessons, you consented to be given for your soul, its opportunity to break all bonds to previous expression. The soul contains within its nature the consciousness of all systems of mind, body, spirit and soul activity of earthly existence.   Your soul's raiment is of light; your soul's consciousness is mind. Within this plane lies the record of all of your experiences.

Follow the meditation procedure:

Once again, experience self in the plane of your own inner mind, unlimited and unbounded by any conditions. Perceive that all awareness is moving into the crown chakra of the Radiant Golden Ray. Let go of all concepts of resistance to the vibration of your own higher knowing.

Perceive now the radiance of this Golden Light and its sound is balancing the body, uniting all that is within and bringing it into focus with the **conscious self.** Know the energy of the light is raising up all held in the physical body bringing it into a higher vibration, spiritualizing **physical matter** into an essence where all is one with the higher self and soul body of light.

At this point, you work within the **causal nature** of the soul. It is here you move by thought and actualize within this dimension any form you desire to express.

As the work takes place within the soul causal body, its activity is beyond the conscious plane and the intellect. In these sessions of light, you are lifted into a different dimension where the soul's essence becomes immersed and enveloped in light and what is unnecessary to carry forth is dissipated.

**Affirm: The will of the soul causal body
releases any conditions opposing unity and love.**

The karmic cause and effect comes into focus through many lives awakened to the spirit. As you have come through many levels within this work of light, you already accepted you are clearing conditions of experiences and balancing this life, healing others as well as yourself.

In your individual journey, you come to that inner healing where you recognize you are less than you desire to be, but greater than you have ever known you could become.

Now receive the guides and masters. There are many teachers and Presences of light, energy and thought, connected to you for the purpose of providing protection.

Perceive the soul moving out of the physical systems. As you rise into the higher planetary dimensions, out-of-body experiences take place. Your awareness rises into this plane of activity and the eyes perceive the physical through higher vibrations. In this plane, there is no separateness. There is only recognition of acceptance of all things as part of an on-going journey. This takes you through many avenues of experience. ...

The Akashic Record is a vibrational consciousness of your individualized soul's journey through time. Within those journeys, the process of evolution manifests.

**Affirm now; any connections holding you in
negative karmic law reveal themselves.**

If your see, feel or recognize life forms, surround them in the light of the Golden Ray. Be thankful for those experiences and expressions for they have played a part in your process to awakening.

The Law of Reincarnation is in constant activity until an initiate transforms and becomes awakened to the Cosmic Consciousness as within the Christ Light. ...

Let the past be and let the now come into its fullness.

Planetary Network

Perceive now the earth enveloped in the rays of this Golden Light. Take this moment to experience rays of energy radiating from within to without, until you become fully one in the network of light. See and feel the Radiant Silver Light as it brings nurturing into mass mind consciousness.

As you direct energy of light to others, so does your own conscious self become uplifted into a higher finer vibration.

...

Go deeply into the journey and travel through time and space becoming as light. Visualize the earth becoming reborn into a total new being, refreshed and purified as in its first stage of evolution.

Man has evolved through many stages and is now entering a new cycle of human development into a spiritualized consciousness. Perceive all nations within the human system accepting the laws of the hierarchy to bring a rebuilding of new consciousness into the human experience. Know we of the hierarchy desire to communicate to bring all nations into recognition of their participation in other systems of life.

It is difficult, for there is yet blindness in many leaders who stand as power and seek to overrule the greater purpose of the evolving human consciousness. However, we do perceive as this new age moves on and becomes fully realized, a plan will emerge from the leaders of the nations and there will be a new order brought into manifestation.   It all begins with the Christ Consciousness awakened and humanity turning to a higher consciousness.

Fear not, nor judge yourself minute and without importance, for there has been much clearing in the soul and in all dimensions of self. Be of simple mind and faith. Magnify the light to dissipate any resistance within the lower bodies.

Let the soul now disengage itself from all negativity, and become fully enveloped in the vibrations of light. Affirm you are one with the Christ Spirit in consciousness, in desire, in service and you are now experiencing within all aspects the Law of Release.

The symbol for the new age is a Radiant Six-Pointed Star linking together the consciousness of all aspects of self, physical, emotional, mental, perceptual, astral and soul. The Star of David symbolizes The Christ manifesting to free all entities from the wheel of karma, rebirth into the Law of Grace. Again, the intellect cannot fully grasp the significance, but let the unfolding process be your confirmation.

Accept now, the cause that brought your soul into the earth is revealed to you. Karmic entanglements are resolved through love. The work continues both in your individual lives and on a planetary scale. You are a part of all those who seek to express the greater good. Feel your soul enveloped in the vibrations of peace. Inner peace comes during the point of clearing past conditioning and consciousness.

Move with awareness back into the physical body.

Pyramid Light Work

Experience once again the light and healing at this level of awareness. Perceive once again the magnetic field vibrating in pyramidal forms and draw within this pyramid all of those who are a part of your life's expression. See each one awakening in their own moment to their own path.

Fear not, nor judge yourself minute and without importance, for there has been much clearing in the soul and in all dimensions of self. Be of simple mind and faith. Magnify the light to dissipate any resistance within the lower bodies.

Once more bring into your own pyramid those who are a part of your life. Hold each in the energy of the pyramid you create for e healing.

. . .

When you have completed your pyramid healing bring awareness back and ground the energy through your own Black Power Ray.

Message & Meditation #2

Trust, as an entity of light you are experiencing all that is necessary for this particular exploration of soul integration. Light and love is the Source. You have nothing to hide.

You are a divine spark of energy that is ready to respond to a perspective of new thought and new ideas. Your soul is becoming a raiment of new vibration actualized in the frequencies of light, but enveloped in Mind yet individualized sparks of its own desire. Desire brings you into effect from not only the present moment, but from time past.

In this moment, the vibration of the energy of the Golden Ray magnifies to uplift and heal the inner causes holding the rage of resistance and pain. Think of your soul connected to journeys of many past life experiences in which it felt insignificant, denied, confused, unawakened, brought to nothingness and devastated under the burden of guilt.

Perceive the cause the soul explored coming from desire to know, in knowing falling into the webs of total third-dimensional consciousness. Your soul enveloped in the causes of the whole human race, experiences itself separated from its divine consciousness.

As initiates, walking through this particular pathway of light, you are to clear the karmic experiences holding you in bondage to pain, suffering, denial, resistance and fear. Individually you will begin to image the soul of yourself in pageantry of time civilizing certain activities within the earth.

As the image is perceived in consciousness, as impulse and as instinct, hold this image and see it inflamed in the Radiant Golden Ray. That which stands as a barrier to its pure image, let it go.

Let go of the slave, and the anger and rage of the slave. Let go of the jester, who found mockery rather than joy. Let go of the woman who bears all the pain of sickness, death and children dying. Release the soul to the light. Disentangle from moments of guilt attached these experiences. Know these effects created through the human system are in the process of their own transformation.

The warrior battles and loses his life under banners of political confusion. Perceive this part of soul also releasing the hold of terror and rage upon itself, know through transformation of life comes a new phase of its desire.

The process within this system of the light brings you from the depths of despair, fear and rage within the soul to a point of creating a new manifestation of peace and love. Surrounding you are those who attach to your vibration from recognition and joy in a process of healing and learning. Many spiritual teachers walk beside you as you begin these inner journeys to unleash yourself from karmic activity.

I, Andrew, come as an emissary under the direction of the Order of Melchizedek; the Prince of Peace and Christ personified in the life as Jesus. I am here as a spokesman from this high order to act as an integrator of light and love to those ready to experience the impact of spiritual consciousness upon their being.

You have all come with an open heart and an open mind. We shall journey together through this round of lessons and you must be patient with yourself as you begin to unlock the hidden doors and depths of desire unexpressed.

To discern between that which is of greater good and that which is destructive to yourself, you must observe which desire brings about a sense of inner peace and a sense of giving to life. Discern what desire explores that which can transform another into a higher expression, and what desire hides self from this inner being and portrays only its vanity. The vanities of your own being will arise to distort you and to change what you know as the direction of your inner intent. This, too, must come to the surface in order for recognition and release.

The power of this moment never can fully be comprehended. Receive now the rays of the Golden Light, magnified intensely upon all vibrations.

Vibration broken down into its most minute form is light; sound and frequency actuated and directed by thought and Mind. So you are, in this moment, mind-active intensified and directed with light, and soul accepts itself mirroring its greater good to the outer plane. Be in the silence.

...

Planetary Network

Perceive yourself connecting through the network of light to direct these rays into the earth. The beautiful planet holds many families of light as well as darkness, for there are those of the dark forces.

As the sound of light moves throughout the earth, perceive it ringing clear to the hearts and minds of all who stand unified under the direction of the higher federation, that of the council of the great Order Of Melchizedek. It is time for peace to be earthed. It is time for the awakening to transpire.

Once again, you come to a season in which the Festivals of Light[5] begin to activate and actuate within the council. More and more, as you become awakened to these great sages, the more you respond to the inner stirring of your own heart and to the knowing that peace is truly a vision meeting its moment in time.

Beloved initiates, much work is taking place as we begin the journey back into the level in which you know yourself to exist. With open hands, mind and thought, perceive in this moment that your structures of energy formulate into the pyramidal system simply to reinforce the magnetic field in and about you. The rays of the Radiant Gold, White and Silver encompass you. As you call forth all those who are a part of you see them as the I AM of their own being, heart, mind and body as one.

…

Go in peace and let the light of the Christ come forth from deep within.

---

[5] Wesak Festival

Message & Meditation #3

Isis - from the Hall of Records

It is of such delight to speak through and to come and spend this moment of energy and light with you. It has been extraordinarily helpful to be able to facilitate these lessons of the light. We have observed their experiment and have perceived the subtleties that come through the initiates' efforts in attuning to the soul and to the spiritual self.

I, Isis, come now to help you come closer to your ideal in Mind, thought and in heart. Again, it is most difficult to live the ideal self in the physical plane when the energies surrounding you are distortions of concepts and are not in alignment with what you understand as spiritual intent.   Nevertheless, you are fully committed to move out of your entrapments into a state of being free to pursue your innermost design.

Each of you discovers within this particular time a closer recognition of your own design. Some of you will find there is an extraordinary purpose and intent within.   Others find you feel different. You may seem less objective and more subjective. This is a contemplative state of knowing and accepting your own state of mind. You attune to the resources of your own belief. You are clearly responding to ideals and the truths you have embraced within yourself. The process of the Gold Ray is to help you in the transformations directed within your consciousness.

The essence of this Golden Ray is most beautiful. The hierarchy recognizes it as one of the most powerful of light energies in reference to the ability to change structure and design. Practicing the tools of light is a way to demonstrate what you have accepted and recognized as the base idea of your own existence. So practicing the power of energy is exploring the way to change what has been difficult to love, to change what has been unbearable to understand, to change what has been indigestible to accept and transform it all into excitement and joy.

Changing dullness, the lackluster and the apathy's of life to action, joyful celebration, to life with love, this is the great transformation. It is as though you move out of the cocoon, the warm dark place of development, to the freedom to express your beauty, your light, your color and your free-flowing spirit.

Soul design is a composite of all of the many journeys you have experienced, both in earth and in other activities of life. Soul has many facets of itself it wishes to express. At times, it may seem very different. Be patient with yourself as you explore the different expressions in need of their place in your life.

As I speak, the causal system is responding to the vibrational energies to help alleviate patterns that are without growth, patterns of stagnation, ignorance and fear. You may find within yourself a certain need for rest. Let it be. Accept you need to rest, accept the change as you gently move through different stages.

Pyramid Light Work

We sense concerns, so at this moment, perceive yourself embraced with many who share your apprehensions and desires. Bring what seems to be difficult into the light. The pyramid structures are always empowering to the mind, to the heart and to the physical plane. You may create or build your pyramid.

As you see all who are a part of this moment within the pyramid, gently send thought that others also find balance in their experience. Join in a spiritual awareness for a physical life that reflects the honor and grace, integrity of humanness and the spirit that the humanness reflects.

As I speak, a great silence comes to each and all of you, feeling and hearing the touch of love. Remember there is no task in the earth so small, any challenge so uninteresting or mundane that it cannot be worthy to experience the light. Bring the concerns of your life to the light.

…

Beloved ones, as you are ready, perceive now each and all of these concerns have already been touched. Focus on you and see yourself lifted away from the fear, away from the doubt.

Walk in peace with the head high, with acceptance and pride in your image as love. Walk straight to the path of your curious life. What you cannot understand and know, recognize as an opportunity to learn.

Lesson Fourteen

COLOR RAY: BLUE

The Light of Wisdom

Message & Meditation #1

Activate the meditation procedure until you reach the Planetary Level and the Hall of Records.

The Soul's Desire and Earth Destiny

Masters

We bring to you the light of the Radiant Wisdom Ray. As you envelop yourself in this consciousness, release all conditionings denying you higher knowledge. Direct this energy into the mental plane, into all of the brain / mind consciousness, into the mind cells. Perceive these cells being cleared of false imageries and past patterns. As this electric frequency travels throughout your being, release the anxieties of your consciousness.

**Affirm: the will of my Higher Self manifests in
and throughout my conscious level.**

The words spoken allow you to attune yourself to the inner potential.

You are now dealing with the inner cause of the soul's desire to manifest within the earth at this particular time.

We desire you to experience your self in a plane and level of being where you experience reflections of all of the probable selves that are aspects of your own soul's beingness.

Think in terms of the soul being multi-faceted, experienced in many different life expressions. There are those probable selves that choose to function intricately with the soul's desire. These probable selves bring desire into focus. It is the probable selves, who choose the roles and destiny of the material plane.

Your probable selves seek to unfold, mend, harmonize and dissipate all that has come into its experience from a position of indebtedness. They choose their function in life, their partners, their soul group and their mode of expression through manner of daily living.

As you perceive this image of self, accept it with love, openness and joy. Embrace that aspect of your nature so that it may feel and know the willingness of the egos to be one with its consciousness to accept its journey through this time and space.

Perceive the Blue Wisdom Ray releasing the fears, denials and doubts, freeing your soul and mind to be an expression of light and wisdom. Doubts and fears from past conditions act as a paralysis to action within the present. They take away from your sense of motivation and purpose.

As the Radiant Blue Ray meets these aspects of false-to-fact consciousness, feel the release of all obstacles and blockages to your complete self-expression.

Once you recognize and remove the doubts and fears, you clear the path for the fulfillment of your own individual service and destiny. The work now taking place is beyond the rebirthing of self at the lower planes. This is truly meeting the inner self and blending with its consciousness. Perceive it now fully merged in joy with all of the selves that you are.

Visualize this ray of light directed into the earth plane, into the mental plane of the human system to uplift the fears.

See the rays of energy moving through the network of light and focused into areas of discontent where wars are running rampant. Let your guides draw you to that which is in need of healing.

There are many events now transpiring within the earth that stand as an obstacle to the higher understanding and peace. But, as you are unified with many who seek to bring the greater good into actuality, perceive a sphere of love and peace manifesting in the innermost mind of the human self from the soul plane to its physical counterpart.

Also, in this moment, as you are merged in one consciousness, perceive the Age of Aquarius, The Millennium, or whatever you understand as the movement into a new time period of the earth's evolution, unfolding in its perfect order with a universal principle of enlightened consciousness.

See the planet moving not into a period of self-destruction, but rather into its stage of realignment and its being regenerated by the mind of man as it accepts itself as a living expression of its Creator, rising out of the animalistic stages into God-like ness.

As this comes more into realization, it will recreate an earth activity which reflects the true divinity of itself. But it must begin within the individual soul vibrations. As individuals take up the "cross," here symbolizing the breaking of the bonds of physical karmic activity and the transfiguration of mind, body and spirit, so too will the earth respond in accordance with the new spiritual awareness.

Ground your energy:

As you return to your own inner center. your awareness moves back into its own conscious self. Perceive the body fully balanced in peace, tranquility and light. Go in peace and may the light of the Christ be in and through you.

Message & Meditation #2

As this energy of the Radiant Blue Wisdom Ray magnifies move with it internally through your body. Focus on those imageries within you that **resist** transformation, change, growth, acceleration and joy. Visualize the physical body now responding as though it is in a radiant sphere of energy. Feel your body becoming lighter and lighter.

The lesson of this particular experience is to visualize in this moment all the hues of Blue Light, from the darkest and deepest blue to the lightest, most vibrant, vivid, clear ice blue. These are all the many hues of energy and frequency associated with this particular vibration. It cuts through the doubts, the confusion, and the dark corners of the mind that dwell in the unknown and harbor fear. Let the light move into those imprints within you.

Affirm the presence of your guides and teachers merging with you and experience the lessons for this level of initiation and consciousness.

Your soul expresses itself as a lighted entity raising its consciousness to understand the imprint of what is moving through itself. The soul is actively experiencing the rays directed towards the core of its own unfolding life. This is the core and cause of its consciousness that brought it to itself in the form of human experience.

Its greatest desire is to know itself to be completely free from any form of incompleteness, any bond that chains it to the imprint of resistance, pain, denial, destruction and thoughts of aloneness from its source.

The soul knows only that it exists as an entity brought into existence through a power beyond its own consciousness. It knows itself as a traveler through many spheres of time, space and life expression. It is familiar with the earth through its many multiples of activity, through its cycles of life consciousness and it knows that it has completed certain levels of awareness. But is also blinded to many of the causes that are now in effect, for it is shadowed by the memories that exist in a conscious level that knows only the moment of its birth to its present time. Therefore, the soul cannot reveal to the ego of the personality the fullness of its existence.

I, Andrew, am here to bring about the bridge of awareness from the inner to the outer and from the outer to the exploration of the inner. You become the instruments of receiving imprints and vibrations of light that stimulate your consciousness to associate with certain life experiences.

The exercise brought to you is in the form of a vision. The quest for the vision is stimulated in the moment. The vision may not be revealed until a time period has transpired, but each of you will experience an imprint and vision of another part of you revealing it to be unlocked from the hidden and released to the light.

The travels of your soul from the beginning of time to present have moved through many different explorations. What has been the core desire, what has been the instigator, what has been the one motion, movement and passion of the soul? Is it to know, discover, create, to be divine and to be human, to be associated with those of the hierarchy? It desires to exist in compatibility with the human experience. The human experience has brought to itself all the different pathways, races, creeds, orders of beliefs and realities.

Your belief guides you through the earth, associating you with the realities created by the human mind. You lived in the world and are now setting yourself free of all that imprisons you.

As you envelope in the rays of light, perceive its flow directed from the absolute center of the over-mind to the intellect within the conscious plane. With this flow of light, know that truth exists ever unfolding, discovering yet truths beyond the knowledge gained through the intellect. Let not the battle continue, but see the mind of the conscious self open, receptive and clear.

Your concerns are how you live, how you clothe the body, how you shelter yourself, how you motivate and create in a world that opposes you as a spirit. There are concerns and anxieties of how to love the unloving, how to heal the wounded, how to stand in courage when fear is aroused by all that stimulates the passions of the human self.

To overcome the passions of fear, experience in the moment the flow of light brings peace and comes from higher knowing. Feel the flow entering into each cell within the conscious self and know the soul's desires blend as one.

Do not be in fear of knowledge or see knowledge as the only way to gain wisdom, for that is a misnomer. Knowledge is the tool of the intellect. Wisdom is the tool of the Mind and of the Spirit. Wisdom knows beyond knowledge. It can utilize knowledge and direct its way by observing the decisions based upon knowledge accepted.

In the moment, sense your body fully integrated.

When you return to awareness, it will be like a cloud has been lifted, as though a stabbing pain within the heart has been healed, as though an emptiness and a longing has been completed into a desire of joy. You come into your wakefulness, walk with a lighter foot and clear understanding. As you begin to move back into consciousness, focus on yourself as free.

Ground yourself.   Go in peace.

Lesson Fifteen

COLOR RAY: EMERALD GREEN

The Light of Creativity

Message & Meditation #1

The Crystal and the Altar

Activate the meditation procedure

Perceive all heaviness lifted into the vibrancy of this radiant Emerald Green energy flow. Perceive all bodies cleared of negativity in any form. By thought, release anxieties, worries and any form of self-destructive consciousness bringing it into the light. Direct this energy throughout all physical systems. Take a moment to feel the essence of this particular frequency. See yourself letting go of all holding patterns that resist expansion or stand in the way of your growth creating obstacles to your manifesting creatively.

Feel yourself disconnected from the body until you become the mind, light and the spirit that knows no form, only itself as an individual consciousness. Direct awareness into the Planetary Center as you meet with the Council of light.

Go deep into the silence as you join your own spiritual teacher and the masters, those who are present for this particular experience in soul activity.

...

The Process

Life in the lane of your own enfoldment can become quickened by clearing the patterns of your past expression. We are going to actively present you with an option in this moment.

The option is to move through a dimension in time where you are open to receive the inner vision of past relations to life experience in the physical plane of the earth. Focus on a certain particular life where you created devastation on yourself as well as others. In this present moment, perceive you are an open mind and are able to accept whatever visions apply necessarily to you and release from that experience the chains that are of guilt and burdens of resistance to understanding.

The soul-causal system, intricate in its minuteness, has a very strong need to experience clarity, purity and total acceptance of itself as Divine.

Whether you began in the earliest phases in the consciousness of the most beastly form, or whether you perceive yourself evolved to a grandiose state enraptured with your own power, vanity and greed, perceive you are accepting that validness of yourself and bring it to the light. Place these images on the altar where they are consumed by the fire of purifying consciousness.

Whether you lived in Atlantis, Lemuria, Egypt, Persia, India, the Orient, in Europe or of the Alaskan nature, whatever essence has been a part of your spirit and soul contributing in a destructive plan, perceive it now placed upon the altar of a Crystal Light.

Perceive now, this crystal growing in an emoting light radiating from the depths of the Emerald Green Energy, the creative vibration linked to the soul and spirit of your own consciousness. This creative self desires to balance the scales and all intricate patterns of your spirit. Perceive it now in this light freed from resistance and persecution from death.

Now perceive the soul itself emerging in the masculine and feminine principle. You are one. You are mind, body and spirit, but you are soul created equally, dynamically and magnetically. You are the father, mother and spirit of your own being. You love what you are completely, whether it demonstrates qualities of the nurturer the mother, the inspired creative magnetic self or whether you demonstrate the force and power of the dynamic will. The desire and cause of the inner self is fully active in love. Whichever aspect of your own consciousness you are relating to and experiencing as yourself, you are fully open to this love.

Perceive the energy of the light directed through the network of consciousness linking through the triangles. You do make a difference.

You are fully active in the transformation manifesting from the heart of the human self to the mind of the human self. You are creating a link from the mental plane and the emotional plane of the collective thought of all human systems. You are a link that brings all things into their higher evolutionary pattern. You all are aware that the earth is moving into a changing vibration, a movement into a higher octave in which its frequency will be felt in a totally different environmental system.

You are aware of energies that seem to be different, you are sensitized to these alternative changes of vibration. You are experiencing your bodies expelling the waste and denseness of the past and re-aligning to a higher vibration.

Body changes are signals to the mind by your change in desire. Your desires are no longer what they were. They are from intensity but of a different nature, a different perspective. This is all a preparation for the event of light that will come into the earth. A shift in awareness as well as a shift in the total physical plane occurs during this century. You are sending vibratory frequencies to help the earth blend in a gentle manner. We perceive the shift not only as a climactic change, but a movement that will bring newness on all levels.

Preparations made for you are beyond what you can comprehend. In this moment, simply know you are links to a great cosmic source. While your life may seem minute or confusing regarding actualizing any desires of the ego, this too shall pass. You will find a greater harmony within your life expression.

Perceive the rays of all the cosmic energy magnified and directed to the beautiful earth, to the planet itself. Send it to all the turmoil, disease, disharmonies and devastations of inhumanity. Those starving perceive fed. Those lacking direction perceive them moving towards their greater goal. To all who seem lost, in devastation and pain, perceive them lifted into divine perfection. Visualize all things manifesting as light.

Bring your awareness to your own consciousness and let go of the conditions you absorb. Let go and let the essence of light guide you.

Affirm you stand in perfect balance as though the body itself changed from imbalance to completeness in its polarity. Visualize the feminine and the masculine aspects are of the same weight, the same source, the same action, united and complete.

When you are complete in this meditation, ground yourself.

Message & Meditation #2

Creativity

It is good to speak.

The first cause (the birth of your individual soul) is a relationship to the Creative Mind (God) and the essence of The Oversoul. The Creative Self is a spark within the Higher Mind. Creativity is the manifestation of a principle, an idea, a thought and an image. Creativity has no barriers, it is. It has only to express itself. In the design of creativity's perfection, it unfolds in harmony with the laws of spirit.

When creativity begins to express in images that portray the shadow of life, the darker side of love, when creativity becomes an urge to express the unclear, the deviated image of love, then creation becomes an image of struggle and pain. The cause of the darker side of the creative process results in the karmic patterns.

The shadows of life will always be when duality is the consciousness of the human soul and of the human mind. It is only when duality is overcome and unity or oneness becomes the absolute, that the shadows and darker sides of self will no longer dominate action. Everyone struggles with the shadow of consciousness as well as the light.

You live in dual expression. You become actively a part of the parallel selves. One, the lightened spirit, the loving being, the image of joy, the hope, the principles of divine thought is in its harmonic consciousness. You also become the dual image. The reflection of fear, rage and pain, struggles with strife, challenge and death brings this into the physical experience.

In this level of the lessons of light, you are practicing the understanding of dual consciousness. Hence, you are seeing your lives impacted with certain challenges that have been your individualized pattern. Without the reflection of the struggle, you would not understand how you are caught in the duality of your existence. You are impacted with challenge. You are also hearing, seeing and feeling the more divine spark of your own essence.

You cannot exist yet without the dual responses of life. In the human world duality is your principle of evolution. But the more you become attuned to the angelic self, the more the angelic self becomes the guiding principle of your being, the less you will find duality and the more you will experience unity of spirit and soul, body and mind.

The rays of light, magnified through you, intensified through the soul system at the causal plane, are imbued with the energy of the Emerald Ray. The creative spark that sets your soul into travel of consciousness is this vibration of light.

Hold the thought:

I am creative divine, I am creative mind, I am creative spirit and I am creative imaged in the likeness of my Creator.

I am a traveler in and through consciousness.

I am in guidance towards my ultimate quest for spiritual wholeness and human joy.

Perceive impressions within the Soul Causal Body that sets itself apart from love, enveloped by Divine Love. Experience the conflicts, confusions and disorientation released out of this causal body to the light.

We cannot image in language what is in effect. This must be your response to the experiences that are transpiring now. To speak can only limit the reality.

Once again, beloved ones, let the experience be your source of understanding, the vibration of the light be your truth. Let the inner love connect to all that you are.

To say you have lived long is a truth. To say you were born in the ages past is a truth. To say you will live through other changes of consciousness is a truth. Agelessness is the state of spirit. Time has little relationship to the state in which soul knows itself. Time is only a measure of awareness in the ego at the human level. How remarkable to be conscious of time, to observe the process of your creation in earth and time. Know beyond this dimension of time you can exist and correspond to parallel worlds of life.

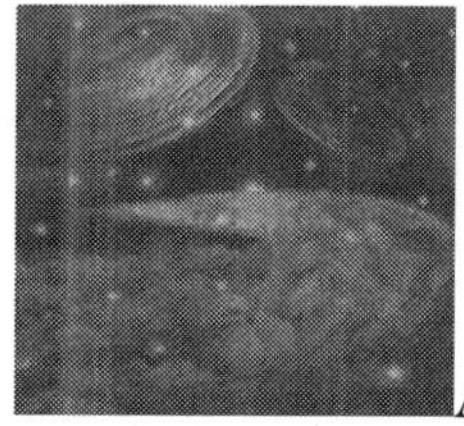

Artist Kathy Nadalin

You travel through time and places to other states in light which images before you other realities you have participated in, as in the reflections of the past and futures of your soul. See your soul not in judgment, but in connection with those that support its path and walk with it through its journeys.

Even in this moment, the healing in effect cannot be measured by time or place, but is explored as an ongoing experience. What is healing in the moment is not realized until you are awakened to its release. What was set in the past may appear in the moment or connect the futures yet explored.

When you awaken in a conscious way, ask that you and all parts of you be fully together in the physical. Love the physical, accept the physical and joyfully connect to the physical.

Visually see yourself awakened fully in the body, touching the earth, grounded to the earth and joyfully accepting your part now. Go in peace.

Lesson Sixteen

COLOR RAY: VIOLET PURPLE

The Light of the Will

Message & Meditation #1

Destiny in the Moment of the Present

Activate the meditation procedure of the soul body of light. Activate each and all centers of light and move awareness into the center of the Violet Purple Ray.

In this moment, let go of thought coming from the mental self of an impure source. Let go of jealousy and envy, thoughts of being confused, lost, alone and disconnected. Visualize thought energy coming from the very center of your soul body of light connecting to the brain creating a vibrant Violet Purple aura around you.

Release all feelings of frustration and discontent from not meeting expectations. Release hurt by expectations you hold as truth but fall short of your intent.

Feel the light and energy from the center of the will of your soul body of light flowing like a beautiful, loving consciousness uplifting the emotions within. Feel the essence of this light touching every level. Perceive and accept the truth frees the fear and brings an internal sense of completeness, peace, tranquility and acceptance.

Once again, whatever conscious patterns and karmic entanglements that hold you in bondage to lack and limitation, freezing your flow of abundance, release these from your consciousness so creative energy may complete its cycle and find its purpose, its place and its fulfillment.

The frequency of this Violet Purple Ray clears away suppressed energy and feelings disconnected from your own internal destined self. Affirm you receive a clear vision to hear and follow what you know as right action.

Know all that you exist as in this moment, is the absolute perfection of your divinity. You cannot see yourself, for you allude to the image of what you see in the mirror of your own reflection. However, as you go beyond the reflection to the inner self, you know from the depth of your heart, you walk as a child of light, as a spirit in this earth plane. You are all the messengers of the light.

You are all, within this light experience, the returning energies and souls who have known this earth as the playground of your spirits many times. You have returned in this time to bring into consciousness one thought, "that light and love is the essence of all being." Light and love is the core that binds one to soul, the soul to the spirit and spirit to the source of its own creativity.

You are in your own individuality manifesting a karmic unfoldment.

Think in terms;   spirit while elusive to thought, is all that thought is, for there is no thought that has no spirit. No one in earth is an empty vessel. The image that a human self can walk in the earth without soul is a fabricated projection that denies the self.

A soul may be hidden, it may be deeply veiled from unconscious impulse and seem to be without life. Therefore, the entity or personality may act from a framework that is totally connected to the animalistic vibration of the human element.

Judge it not. Simply know soul is and lies in the depth of that being. As you raise the consciousness of self to enter into the inner being and to view that soul as light, you quicken the vibration and act as a catalyst to transmute and transform by thought the entity's vibration.

You stir a new process within that individual. Recognize the inner self as the Christ, the Christ as an essence of spirit and love, the Immanuel, the one thought that lies at the core of all entities.

While karmic consciousness is perceived as cause and effect manifesting over and over, as soul you are disconnecting from karmic patterns and repetitions of past errors and judgments.

Accept, whatever lies within your individualized soul and holding you in the tremors of life, as severed in this vibrant energy of the Violet Purple. Perceive light cutting through the cords that bind you to the negative forms of past incarnations.

The thread of history runs through the thread of your own individuality. The manifestations of historical events are imprints within your soul's memory. You identify with certain periods of time where you have actualized as energy in mind and spirit within individual soul consciousness and have performed or lived in different eras of this historical planet of earth.

In this present moment, think all which preceded you in this life, and drew you back into this wonderland of consciousness, is being brought into a full cycle as know you complete in this initiation all that was incomplete. Accept you relate to those who are in need of relating to you, as if there is a perfect synchronicity of consciousness.

Whatever lesson comes before you, visualize it as an absolute perfect fulfillment of cause and effect. When it is a difficult lesson, painful to the eye, the ear, the heart and it tears at the emotions and feelings, visualize that act, has come from a cause for change. Those who cannot see and cannot hear must have their own day of blindness until the light shines upon them.

Each of you are touched once again, as your spirits recognize this communion, this inner activity, this Presence, feel the vibration. Acknowledge its flow to you, through you, as a part of you and extended it outward.

Many questions may exist in mind. *"How much longer is my life to be? When will my life be filled as though I walk without judgment and confusion and know only a source of harmony?"*

Your path, beloved ones, often is a walk with a heavy step and a heavy mind. As you look around and see the injustices of humanity's creative acts, it is almost unbearable. But, each heavy foot walked along this path will surely find its steps lighter as it senses itself in its own narrow corridor of truth.

You all have a destined purpose and some of you will find it quickly. Others will struggle to unfold and to experience it coming as an event. The key is to know that it is already here and you are destiny in the moment.

You will forget, you will always forget, for that is the conscious way to find itself against the wall of fear, denial and separateness. When you come into that blinded spot, do not be angry with yourself or let foolishness ride your actions. Recognize you are in a passage of change. You will see again and you will know again.

This particular level of your initiation influences repercussions from the traumas of the past. It may appear in its own present moment as disassociated from a karmic activity, but in essence, you are processing tremendous actions of past insights, life experiences, acts of discord and despondency. This is all a part of you. The words are forgiveness, release, manifestation, acceptance and love. These steps are the freedom of soul to light and light is Mind.

Perceive now the rays of energy connected through the networking of the hierarchy once again transforming the ill-will rages of human emotion and mind into the joy of acceptance and peace. Where the earth changes and leaves its mark, perceive that too as the beginning of a new earth. All of the old becomes the new. Within the new begins a new evolved state of self, human emotion and human evolution.

Begin to feel yourself moving forward, standing outward, and traveling in and through the network of light. Be a messenger, for the radiance unfolds, uplifting and healing.

As you return to your source, feel your vibration earthing into every particle of your physical body. Do not leave your body. Your body is an important part of how you are truly a manifestation in the now. Your body and you are an instrument, fully and completely in its own perfect action. So, as you move into that realization through your body, see it once again as an extension of your total self.

Message & Meditation #2

We wish to relay the experiences now in effect, both through you individually and through the preparation for the influx of the cosmic light to the human ego systems.

Energy, as you are discovering, is most beneficial to many situations of creation. Energy of light, through the awareness of its presence, can be adapted to many different needs. You are going to find need factors of your ego systems replenished with light. Conscious self can explore the light in many ways, through thought, through vision, through touch, through smell, through hearing, through just sensing. You will find each and all of the properties of light as energy can be actually focused on to bring about change in the system of the physical world.

You have been finding yourself in transforming stages, attributing it to the process of awakening to the ill, awakening to the right to be healed, awakening to the desires for change, awakening to the ultimate acceptance of your worthiness to live in freedom, joy and peace. You have been awakening to the right to exist in God-like consciousness as well as the exploration of the human self. All in all, your processes of awakening have touched upon the deep roots of your total creation.

Now you are wondering how can you enhance what is awakening in your self. How can you best demonstrate light so that others can tap into its resource? How can light and energy be demonstrated in scientific ways or in practical terms? How can it be developed, in scientific communities, acknowledged and accepted as a part of the spiritual demonstrations of love and God-consciousness?

You find science itself looks to energy and light as true realities. Exploring these frequency bands you are noting many changes in the usage of these bands of light. Through instrumentations, you are seeing it in technical systems as enhancers for clearing and breaking through disease.

You are seeing the usage of light in many different facets for human growth, for understanding and for wellness of the body. You are also seeing it as an aspect of interest in the utilities or the usage of energy in utilitarian ways. So, you are finding the age of the next cycle of life more focused to the energies of light, for you are in the right time for these explorative demonstrations.

Now the planet earth is in need of light in many ways. Light is needed through the mental self, directed through you as souls to enhance the clearing process of the pollutions that have blocked and failed the clarity of the atmosphere of the earth. There is a need for light energy for planet earth in ways to enhance rejuvenation properties of life species. Light energy is a need to change the consciousness of the human ego systems. Light energy soon is recognized as a universal manifestation of creation. Light energy is in need of love to demonstrate its power to restore wholeness to the bodies and to the species of life in the earth's evolutionary system. The sharing of the lightwork is through many different sources.

Visualize

Therefore, in the frequency ray associated with the will, the enhancer of divine intent, the enhancer of demonstrations of the destined path of the Good will, perceive you are networking with a band of consciousness. Perceive many multitudes are gathering in focus to help manifest and initiate the light in and through the mental body of the earth, the mental aura that surrounds the earth planet and the combined consciousness of the awareness of all that lives. Perceive this mental body of the earth enveloped with the rays of this Violet Ray of energy. Focus on the will of the highest order of creation recognized, accepted and appeased by the egos that lead the earth.

Perceive the rays of this light as responding to the call of the inner heart of the human family to be free. Focus this light on those imprisoned without justification, those in the hostage place, those in political arenas that have no human choice to be free. Focus on the power of love and the power of divine will to break through the illusions and the rages of the misappropriations of truth. Perceive that what has been in war is resolved into peace, into change, into growth, into rebuilding and into newness.

Perceive whatever orders for human development have been established be surrounded and attuned to this energy to help expand the vision, to help grant growth without restriction in order of divine law.

Perceive what has been ill created through ignorance and fear meet the corresponding energy of wisdom and love. Perceive a new order of understanding comes into the egos of the family of birth.

All the ills of life in karmic law have causes in need of healing. We cannot know the causes of all the ills of the shadows of the ego systems, but you can know the power of love and you can focus and image this power changing.

As this work is in effect, so is this work within you individually in motion. For what is demonstrated for growth is connected to the inner, and all is in its own fine order now. We are working very clearly with you as you begin the work to help clear others in their needs. There is much to be shared and explored.

Let go of thoughts of your individual struggle. Let go of thoughts of being incomplete. Accept what is given to you to live by, to grow by, to explore, will be met.

We wish the link and bonding of this consciousness to be a continuous experience for many times ahead. Know you are connected and are part of many who link to the light.

Do not fear that this is against other forms of belief. Perceive it as the understanding that allows the meeting of the minds of many to come together equally with truth, clarity and peace.

Direct all of the egos comfortably through to the body, ground and integrate the lesson. Go in peace.

Lesson Seventeen

COLOR RAY: RUBY RED

The Left Hand of the Physician

Message & Meditation #1

The First Cause and the Inner Temples

Follow the meditation procedure:

Artist Kathy Nadalin

Open the eyes of the soul that you may see the beauty that envelops you. For you are in beauty and you are radiant lighted souls seeking to understand your service in life. Open your vision where you may perceive *the temple beautiful* and its perfect light. Many journey into this plane to communicate with the angels of their own being, experiencing the revelations of their spirit. You see in accordance with the openness of Mind to accept the vision.

Each ray of light can become a form that reflects much of what you see in your own earth. We have spoken how the many temples on earth are reflections of what is contained within these dimensions lighted dimensions. The *temple beautiful* is a place which soul comes to experience communion with masters and the spiritual dimension. In this place of light, you remove the effects of difficulties and strife of physical conditions. The body becomes dis-eased, and soul becomes weary losing strength, with stresses and conditions of earth. Within this level, light energy envelopes the soul in vibrations of light for healing and renewal.

You each are moving to the causal-desire factor of your own nature and system. You are reaching a stage where you are letting go intensities of karma that brought your first cause into earth experience. This requires some explanation.

A *soul cause* first developed its imbalance in previous life experiences. Acts and deeds against another individual, for the sake of self-preservation and wealth, can cause intense distortions of the soul's true spiritual creation. Pride, authority, greed and conflict can cause within the soul a loss of its integrity and perfected self. Therefore, the soul meets what it creates through recurring actions.

As each of you have incarnated through many journeys and different life expressions. Soul has within itself many attachments, energy patterns which act like magnets, drawing reflections of these forms into physical likeness. Those you meet in moments of fear may be those souls previously encountered out of acts of unworthy activity.

As you enter into these *inner temples* the guides and teachers of the Council of Light magnify the healing energies to stimulate the soul out of its difficulty into a clear vibration.

In time, the outer life begins to reflect this by a less heavy, less burdened body and an overall less-stressed mental and emotional condition. Then the outer life begins to function as a free spirit adventuring through life with only a sense of pure joy and love. It feels its attachments as a new experience free of karmic activity. Yet as you live within the earth, you cannot move without the challenges and struggles before you.

As these challenges and tests are met, you will be perceived by others standing clear crystal, seeing with new eyes, experiencing everything with a freedom of mind unburdened by guilt and pain.

Therefore, perceive your soul enveloped in the vibration of light and the beautiful healing rays of the heart chakra. Let the soul experience this vibration as a rose, perfect and fragrant. Release from any memory within the mental or emotional systems all experiences of harm.

It has been spoken the soul is to be washed in the blood of the lamb. The blood reflects the life force, the lamb symbolizes the innocence of life and the purification comes through birth into new consciousness. Each of you let this experience be your conscious knowing.

You may ask, *"What is destiny? What is fate? When does the conscious mind know of its destiny and its fate?"* Know you are walking the destined paths of your intent.

As minute as your contribution may be to the service of life, it is still an important part in the total pattern of the earth and your individual soul's evolution. Your contributions are the transformations taking place within and around you. Each thought you give to heal brings healing within self as well as to others.

Therefore, move out of thinking you are minute and without effect and know your living consciousness is love in action.

Let your physical selves be in peace and commune in silence within this dimension. Each of us, within the Order of Melchizedek, work as one consciousness to raise our earth brethren into higher levels of evolving thought and spiritual integration. Yet, each works individually.

You are all acquainted with the techniques given previously. They are an important part of your self-knowing for they are aspects of your own soul's consciousness.

When you are ready return back to the source of your conscious self, the thought will bring it into action.

We are most pleased for each soul who experiences the light in their personal progression. Know there are no miracles; there is only the law. It may escape the understanding of the intellect, but behind each action, there is *a principle*. Therefore, know all is in its proper order and let the flame of this Radiant Ruby Red energy bring peace to the spirit, soul, mind and body.

Message & Meditation #2

Feel yourself embraced by the consciousness of your own guides and teachers, by those who are within your family, your soul family and your human family. Thoughts and memories lay deep in the unconscious that experienced alienation from the source of its own spirit. Feel now the energy of light and release this alienation and separateness from memory. Let feelings rise to the surface, experience the light integrating within all the emotional consciousness. Accept this vibration as it lifts the frequency level of your body, your consciousness and all that you are.

Clear away all doubts, all anxieties. Once again, whatever you doubt, you experience. You release the doubt and you experience something new. Feel this center open wide and let go of the fear of loss of your own being, let go of the fear of the power of others. Feel the source of strength within you. Whatever this dimension feels like, experience yourself in the presence of beautiful teachers, guides and counselors, who connect to your consciousness through thought, energy and mind.

The life you live is the life given to you to explore every part of what your soul desires to emanate. In this plane and dimension of consciousness, you are active in a manner you cannot fully focus on, but the soul itself is directed. It is receiving from sources beyond the intellect. Grasp what it must manifest in order to become free from its entangled selves.

Think in this moment you are in a *hall of mirrors* and each mirror reflects an aspect of continuous life experiences, as though you are mirroring many images from the past ages into the present time. Each phase, each identity, each energy form and each personality system is enveloped in the purity of light and in the rays of healing consciousness.

Focus now in the frequency of the Radiant Ruby Light, which brings awareness of the desire to complete your physical life, healing the lives presented to you in this *hall of mirrors.*

Within this *hall of mirrors*, find yourself in the silence reflecting on all the lives your soul experienced. In this moment, acknowledge that all of these participating egos were a creation of itself and whatever pains, whatever wounds, whatever harms, whatever destroying focuses have been portrayed, now place it upon the altar in which the light enfolds the memory and heals whatever scars exist in the depth of soul systems.

There is no scar so deep that spirit, as love cannot heal. There is no act committed that cannot be balanced throughout the eternal cycle of light. Respond to this with a humble heart, loving self, loving Your Creator and loving all you know.

You are a star amongst stars; you are a point of light amongst many lights. You are an individualized mind, unique and perfect of itself. Within this mind lie resources of your ability to act out your true destiny. The total purpose of this particular level is to claim yourself as ready in consciousness to experience the Law of Grace.

Think of healing rays, as the symbol of all life forms. As your vibrations lift the past wounds within the soul record, perceive your light merges with the great host of beings. The greatest healing is what you give back to life.

In this moment, once again perceive yourself as a radiant healing light magnified and directed into the earth. Accept those who cannot see or hear are yet touched in the heart of their own being experiencing a direct effect of the light.

You make a difference in the moment. You make a difference in the rays you emanate. You touch the unknown as well as the known, for thought is the instrument of the healing focus.

There are many changes transpiring, many changes in the earth beyond even what you have even considered. There are changes in the internal structure and the core of the earth, changes in the activity of the human element, changes in the national international, political and economic focus. Changes are all around as there is movement towards resolution from long held rages.

There are those who revolt against change and terrorize creating war, holding hostages and creating loss of lives. There are those who stir the waters of turmoil and create the storms of pain, but they are fewer than what has emanated in the past.

What is an internal and external crisis is moving beyond the first impact. A nuclear holocaust is becoming a faded image. It no longer is a crisis on the forefront of the absolute. Yet, there always is an incident that can arise. From the perspective of how we perceive the evolution of man and spirit, we see man moving beyond the need to annihilate his existence and create a new vibration in which an element of love is truly the core of activity.

Law and discipline become tools that gain precedence within factions of different social systems. We are most pleased as we begin to perceive a new phase of communication emanating between individuals, group to group, from network to network. A new sense of community is evolving as more understand the light and give way to the inner calling.

You, as individuals, in this precious moment of your own life, feel your inner body and know you as soul, is standing on the threshold again of a new phase of your own awareness. Look at yourself with joy, look at your being with love, look at your total nature with acceptance. Look at you as though you have completed a tremendous task of evolution to a consciousness of higher activity. You are moving and the movement is in a pace of extreme acceleration.

As you begin once again to move back into your own physical plane, move into the dimension of your awareness of self and feel the consciousness of light in the pyramidal structures of energy.

Bask in the light and allow integration until every part of your body, every tiny cell and every organ within self feels the vibration of healing. Your body responds with openness, acceptance and perfection.   Go into silence and bring those into the pyramid you desire healed.

Go in peace and may the light of the Christ be in and through you.

Lesson 18

COLOR RAY: ORANGE

The Right Hand of the Physician

Perception and Sensitivity

Message & Meditation #1

Mind and Desire

Activate your meditation procedure.   As your have gathered your egos and consciousness into the soul body of light visualize in this moment the mental aura, the collective thoughts all enveloped in rays of light.   Let go of conscious thoughts focused on doubts, fears, separateness, anxiety and resistances. Experience the light healing and cleansing your body, releasing you from the old patterns of mental thought that stir you into negative reactions.

Whatever feelings exist from within you, experience the light enveloping them all.   The beautiful ones as well as the negative feelings surround them in the light.

Release any psychic attachments you have holding you in a state of anxiety, hypertension or fear clouded by illusion.   Ask that perceptions and instinctive feelings are absolute clarity.

Envision this light magnified and brilliant.   Direct its frequency into the body, merging with brain /mind thinking.   The frequency of this light stimulates all the tiny cells in your own brain. Perceive your consciousness connected to a positive energy flow, to a positive system where you begin to know yourself functioning in absolute perfect design with the inner and outer consciousness.

Focus in this moment on who you are, what you desire to be, your objectives and goals. Perceive it all balanced and in harmony.

I affirm that I am clear and free.

Moving into the planetary center, merge with your inner guides and counselors. As you enter into the *Hall of Records* and into the silence commune with the presence of your inner being. Open your mind to explore the sound, the touch, the feel and the awareness. Light as you know, is the source in which consciousness flows and travels in and through all the spheres.

In the decades to come, you will travel to the stars in vehicles that have attained the ability to function in absolute accord with light. Before that comes into its full exploration, there is the necessity for experiencing the ultimate understanding of Mind and its connection to the forces within the universal experience.

Therefore, beloved students, in this moment focus on yourself as Mind expanded beyond the minuteness of your conscious thought. Think of Mind (God) as the developer, the divine love connected to spirit within and without all activity.

Focus on yourself as a part of this Mind. Within this Mind, visualize and perceive what you desire to be. Hold the image of you actualized completely in your innermost desire. Ask the cause of this desire to acknowledge itself, to stimulate and process all that is necessary to create its reality. Envision within Mind (God) your individual soul. It merges, it expands, it can be formless or formed, for it is much like Mind, its awareness is always present.

When you move beyond the physical dimension into this plane you are much like your consciousness making transition from the physical vehicle to the spirit world. Just as you now are aware that you live, move, breathe, exist, touch, feel, see, behold and emanate, your soul is all of these aspects of consciousness.

Perceive now that you move to a point within the universe. Think, exist, acknowledge and become. Research where you are, what are the sounds? What star do you wish to explore? What galaxy do you wish to travel? What being do you wish to meet? What sphere do you wish to encounter? What do you research? All of these are your tools of consciousness.

Thought directs, thought follows the flow and moves with the flow and becomes the force within itself. You are spirit and mind, and soul is the form in which these exist.

The soul bound by the incompleteness of its karmic journey must respond to the lessons and challenges of the dimension in which it exists. Within the light, soul experiences itself looking in the perspective of its past creations and acknowledges the need to balance the imbalances. So, in this moment, once again forgive the soul's unknowingness in actions, attachments and places. Perceive its understanding fully awakened to itself and its identity.

There are those who would teach that the soul needs no purging or purification, yet you are bound to the earth by the unfulfilled design and the interactions resulting from causes of your creative desires. Not all desire is an expression of the greater good. Desire can create destructive forces. Purging is a necessity to bring self through the process to its own clarity.

In the now, sense that you are enveloped in light and light responds as a medium to bring into motion the clarity on all levels of your existent self. Ask that your inner vision and knowledge of your consciousness responds within the earth plane. Perceive the egos of the body and the forces of your lower self experiencing an awakening and heightened sensitivity.

You have accepted through belief and knowledge the experience of this process. Therefore, you have come to a plateau where your belief and acceptance become a manifestation objectified in perfect order within your life.

You no longer are bound in karmic entanglements. There is less of yourself attached to resistance.

Perceive you become a vibrant force, acknowledging a need to heal those who suffer under great loss in confused lives and the turmoil of storms. Accept and know that the earth and its inhabitants can live in harmony when the karmic bondage of the past is no longer a necessity.

The ancient tribes echoing from the past still stand as forces clouding the human evolution. So many lives are released within these time periods in order to be placed in another dimension for a higher development of their individual self. Begin to sense the healing occurring in the open wounds in which despair and death overshadow the joys. Perceive famine replaced by supplies and acknowledge shelter for the wandering ones.

When you have completed your inner work and once again desire draws you back to the body, perceive the activation of the pyramid structure around you.

How you create the pyramid structure is now in the thought of your higher self. As you feel pyramid of energy surrounding you bring into this field of light those of your life. Bring into this sacred space those who reach out for love and healing. Bring into this space those whom you are clearing from your pain. Hold yourself in silence.

When you are aligned, healed and blessed, you will feel the peace within yourself.

Ground your thoughts, your spirit and your light through the Black Power Ray and anchor your consciousness.

Lesson Eighteen

COLOR RAY: PINK

The Light of Balance and Perfection

Message & Meditation #1

The Soul and the Living Christ

Soul is most complicated for the soul has the existence of itself from many eons of time. Even in its individualized embodiment, it is a composite of different energies, experiences of time and life. Your soul cannot be seen, touched, felt or proved to exist by science. Yet, evidence of the soul experiences a consciousness beyond brain-wave activity, beyond the heartbeat, beyond the sensory and life forces of the body does exist.

As life fades from the physical and transits into another form, the experience of separation is most universal. It evades the scientific element and yet, it is correlated time and time again, that a living, breathing, knowing consciousness cannot be held fixed as only three-dimensional matter, but is recognized as something beyond what is of human consciousness.

In this meditation, your soul expands and your awareness of yourself is centered in this plateau where you are one with many lighted ones, guides and teachers of the Council of Light. Experience yet another phase of initiation and clearing within this dimension.

Again, we cannot individualize your soul's memory, but at this moment, we desire you to think of your own individual soul record as in the Akashic Record, the Book of Life. This record is the living essence of all that you know as your existence in life both within and outside of the earth dimension.

Perceive and accept there is perfect order and divine intent through all these life experiences, not judged with the human intellect, but understood with spirit and mind.

Within these inner *halls of learning*, the teacher of your own being approaches. Ask what is necessary to understand in order to fulfill the unfulfilled, to resolve the unresolved, to balance the unbalanced and to clear that which would hold you in states of confusion and pain. Perceive self as breaking through the veils of your higher being.

As you move in and through your daily activities you will find a greater order and less burden on your physical senses.

We speak of the Master Christ so that you may once again experience His vibration. The love energy brought to the earth through His consciousness remains and is still outpouring to all within the realm of acceptance.

It is a matter of finding His Light and attuning yourself to its frequency. Accept the truth, He is the Master Teacher of teachers, the Healer of healers and the spirit of the Christ, which emanates the creative consciousness individualized through Jesus. This energy is still active within the earth as well as the inner planes and is always a constant Presence.

The living masters, recognized as the teachers in the earth plane, have descended from the hierarchy and have their work to do, creating pathways for disciples to follow in order to experience their own self-knowing. They come not to interfere, discourage or deny these pathways as a means to self-unfoldment. They come simply to re-state, you are one under the Council of Light under the overseer of the Christ Spirit and the Presence known as Jesus.

As workers in light, you bridge the understanding between the limited view of the actualized life lived 2,000 years ago and your understanding of the Living Christ.

Beloved students of light, as you have been in communion with the teachers of your own consciousness, focus upon divine love, the Radiant Pink Ray as the key to balance. Move with your own awareness and direction back into the vibration of your own physical plane. Feel a clearing as though the coming together of the soul to the physical is more harmonious and there is an easiness and completeness.

Feel each center vibrating and its rays of light expanding outwardly to bring love into the environment in which your daily lives take place. … silence

Connect with the network of light and visually see that the divine Love energy is connecting each and all sending its vibration into the earth

Ground your consciousness as you come back into your body.

Go in peace and may the light be in and through you.

Message & Meditation #2

Wesak Festival

Each year during the full moon of June, there is a gathering of Councils of Light and the brotherhoods of Ascended Masters.

Welcome, beloved students, welcome initiates, welcome light workers of all the earth that exist as a part of the universe. Welcome to the Wesak Festival, a gathering of the councils of Ascended Masters. We concur together during this full moon in the month of June to bring directives for the age that moves into the dawn of its unfoldment.

The council is called to gather at this time to project the vibration of this Perfection Ray and prepare the heart chakras of the human race to experience an awakening of the purity of love. As you envision the earth and all that dwells within, perceive that nothing outside of divine love can have the power to shut the door on the inversions of love. Perceive the total earth and what dwells within it, beats with a heart that knows its center as a perfected image of its own creation and Creator.

There comes a time when all shall be in joy, transformed and uplifted, beyond what any mind can comprehend. You receive a glimmer and experience now, a minute part of that ecstasy of light. As you hold this experience within you and call its memory to self again, accept it as a total reality for you. Deny it not; see it as it truly is. You participate in a beautiful celebration, a celebration in which the power of love is coming into a fuller realization on all planes.

Yes, you experience the opposition to this divine intent. Yes, you see in all that the earth expresses in itself, what appears as negative systems, but recognize it is all a passing through of past karmic realities.

There truly is a day in which the greater activity transpires within and around you. Within the centering of yourself into that inner balance, visualize in the now all who dwell in the mind and the spirit, in the physical, in the creation, become touched to extend the power of love into all humanity. You serve wherever you are, where you walk, where you speak and where you act. Where you experience yourself is where the light becomes an eminence.

As you are focused within the Radiant Pink Ray center, experience the energy expanded into a radiant sphere. All of your thoughts and collective energies creating projections of being incomplete, out of balance, off-center, abandoned, rejected, denied and unloved, release them to this Radiant Pink Light

Acknowledge you are a complete individualized Mind, manifesting in action throughout your conscious experience.

Let go of all feelings in the heart causing disorder and disharmony. Ask for clarity within your instinctive, intuitive and perceptual consciousness. Feel this light energizing, transmuting negative mental patterns that react from confusion and disorientation. Feel these patterns severed from within yourself and focus on creating positive mental images surrounding your desires, your goals, your objectives and your destinies. Put aside all doubts regarding your abilities, your creative nature and ask for action.

Once again, let go of any fears regarding your ability to create. Release those obstacles that leave you feeling imprisoned, restricted and denied. Visualize yourself acting in perfect order with your own sense of purpose and goals. Visualize yourself as you desire to be, completing the inner work and acting outwardly in a manner in which you feel your call to express.

You receive direction of your inner and outer expression. All you have been preparing for is on the dawn of your spirit's acceptance of light. You are that which is to be the implanted seeds of the coming time in which change evolves under a direction of a cosmic order.

As you work to explore the nature of your own being, confirm and know yourself as light, as a perfect crystal of healing activity.

Focus and flow with this vibrant energy that brings balance and order throughout the networking of light surrounding the earth for the healing of the earth planet.

Perceive that with the Council of Light, you experience the networking activating this radiant sphere of energy. Let the balance come from within, sending it outward. In this level, perceive the soul of your individuality wholly enveloped in this ray of light and the desires of itself coming into fullness, actualized, present in form, balancing the creative process on all levels of your endeavors.

...

Continue with your networking of light.

As you come back into your physical awareness, activate the pyramids of light.

Perceive your consciousness activating the pyramids of light. The advanced stages of this particular level are creating within you an internal acceptance of your inner spirit where you perceive your outer life without fear.

Activate the pyramids of energy for you to gather all who are connected to your life, drawing them to share from the heart vibration of healing and the vibration and spirit of love.

...

In completion, direct your awareness to the physical plane to become conscious of your own body, when you awaken you will feel internal changes as though your structures are in perfect order.

Walk with the light and go in peace.

Lesson Nineteen

COLOR RAY: AMETHYST

The Light of the Peaceful Warrior

Message & Meditation #1

The Council

We greet you in the name of The Spirit of the Christ, the overseer of that which you are, for you are all a part of the many souls that are part of the armies of His own bands of energy.

The call of Christ has come. Those who are intensifying their acceleration are feeling the bond to this force and are experiencing the need to move forth into the true expression of their higher self. The coming is imminent as manifested into the earth system. Those who recognize its vibration are feeling the necessity of creating the proper order for the service and for the work to unfold.

The Christ Spirit is unbound through all who are willing to see its activity of wholeness. The manifestation of the Christ Consciousness is coming into many who are ready to let go of the shackles of past negation, to let go of the bondage of past incarnations and to let go of all the chains of past life activity.

In this particular experience, again we focus on the embodiment of light, the essence and soul of all that you are, not to divide you or separate you from a sense of wholeness, but simply to reflect on what the soul is seeking to manifest in this particular time and initiation.

Through this planetary level of the path of *A Course in Light*, you gather into the soul system where the Akashic Record is exposed.

In these light experiences, you are disentangled from past karmic activity and the healing on the soul plane is intensified.

Each time you experience a releasing of past regret, each time you experience a forgiveness of past negations and each time you experience a release from systems that bind you to negativity, you are clearing the soul energy. You are clearing the consciousness of the soul's attachment to systems that deny the truth. Each time you experience an integration of love, each time you experience an influx of spirit, you are strengthening all factors within your own being.

You have read the words of the Masters and you have filled the intellect with its understandings of how the soul is in a pilgrimage through its journey of experience. It desires to completely reunite with its first state of being. Through eons of time, it has left its original state and moved through different consciousnesses and planes of activity,. The awareness in which you exist in the present moment is in the plane of the soul, the fifth dimension of consciousness.

You may ask, *"How does one complete a karmic debt? How does one resolve unfinished business? How does one turn the key from creations of the past, to the future and to the now?"*

We say by recognition and by knowing. To know thyself is to be free, to know thyself is to be open to look into the indebtedness of past life experience and to allow the light to ease you through what challenges you on the physical plane.

Again, we cannot take away that which you came to express. We can uplift and lighten your being so that you may choose and discern with the higher knowing and with a clearness of mind and direction.

For each soul consciously expressing a vibrant life, utilizing its healing and manifesting from its source of love, there are still many more in a state of need. For each soul involved in their own transformation, there are still many more in a state of need. Therefore, the key is to begin from within and around the self that you know as you. As you have seen on the inner planes, as you stand focused and perfectly centered within the light and it flows in and through your magnetic field, others awaken to that vibration and experience a lift and activity of intense quickening.

Again, each time soul energy connects into a magnetic field where the light is intensified through openness, receptivity, trust and love, there is an awakening taking place and a desire to experience what is coming from that vibration.

In this moment, you are experiencing the frequencies of the Amethyst Light, that which stimulates the warrior nature of your own consciousness. Know there is not one of you who has not walked the battlefield in some activity. Yet, in this life, you choose to lay down the sword and the weapons of the past and to work with the swords of Mind, to work with the knowledge of spiritual truth and to savor your life with new eyes, new expression and new love.

As you are in this vibration, perceive all the warriors of your soul's remembrances accept their place in their incarnating activity. Absorb from this warrior aspect the tenacity of will, the courage, the strength, the discipline and see this warrior as the protector and defender of all that you are and for those brought into your experience for counsel and wisdom.

Again, through conflict comes the resolution. Accept expansion within self and you will reflect it.

Perceive the rays of this energy directed into the mental plane of the earth's consciousness. Perceive thoughts of peace, balance, oneness and harmony received and meditate on all within the earth. Perceive this energy directed into the diseases within the bodies of the human system, into the ravages of impurities that create illness. Focus upon man as balancing his own thought forms and creations.

Each kingdom is a reflection of a creative process. By kingdom we mean, each life form created from the atom to the universe. Each life form is a miracle of its own consciousness. Yet, its dualities exist within the earth and so the warring factor becomes a part of its lesson learning experience.

The initiate's goal is to reach inner peace by being in harmony with Mind, consciousness and spirit. Perceive the desire of the soul as a creative expression. Ask, "What is the creator of your consciousness desiring to express in the present moment and in its life process?"

Its purpose is to teach, to heal, to love and to attain greater states of freedom and strength.

Perceive the soul body of your individual self once again lifted up into a higher frequency and into a higher expression. Love all aspects of your being. To deny one part is to deny all. Therefore, love not only the soul, but also the physical as well.

A blessing is a recognition of the higher good affirmed consciously. Therefore, send your blessings to each one who is connected to your circle of experience. Bless them to be as their highest expression. Free each one to explore the adventure of unfoldment. Feel the protection of the light as it envelops all systems.

Message & Meditation #2

It is I, Isis. I will give to you a greater understanding of the presence that my spirit represents. (Referring to her own name) A name can only reflect an idea, a vibration or a state of beingness. A name denotes a certain relation of the self to its own inner light or being. Isis is a name associated through history as the feminine god that brings into effect the nurturing qualities of spirit. Isis represents the goddess of perfection in its divine order when it is truly expressing its principle as a creating being.

Each and all who speak through the processes for this course have links to the earth, have lives that were important in the earth and are also linked to those planes of consciousness that teach the way to systems beyond the initiation of earth time.

The Lightwork, as you have been so diligently a part of, is preparing you for a stronger role in the direct of the evolution of the human family. The Council's concern is to prepare each and all inwardly and outwardly for ability to be focused and centered on the reality of light, the principles that govern creation and the design that light initiates in all the ego systems. So we have all participated in observing the processes you walk through and we are all participants in the teaching of this initiatory experience.

It is for me, at this moment in time, to be the dynamic perpetrator of the feminine energy, to harmonize the egos with its intuitive self and to bring the creating consciousness into a more profound expression. You are all important to this experiment of light. You are ancient souls. You have so many different beautiful life experiences within the planet and you are working internally with impressions your soul has absorbed from the trials, the tribulations and the challenges that many earth lives presented.

So in this level, as you call it, you are clearing many deep seated conditions that memory has instilled within the soul. You are working through physical change and all the different bodies. You are each stepping into a different framework of consciousness. It may seem difficult to acknowledge this when in reality of this third world and third plane, you see yourself in obstacles and fear.

It is difficult to see yourself and recognize the goddesses of you when the physical world is bombarding you with your image of limitation, denial and pain. Yet, beloved, you are experiencing each and all of these challenges to help in teaching. You are setting the pace for others whose need for understanding becomes acute. So, be blessed in your pain and grateful for your challenge. Be in light and love the wisdom you are exploring and becoming.

You are seeing much in the planet. You have seen more through your individual eyes and heard more from your individual ears on earth change, than any previous incarnations of soul in human life. You are observing many, accelerated stages of human growth. You are also seeing the complexities that growth has brought into effect. You are observing the imbalances and have set certain crises into motion. Be assured, even through the crisis cycles there is order amongst all that takes place.

You are the pacesetters of holding to the divine. You are the freemasons, you are the eastern stars, you are the soul beings from higher planes of consciousness, you are souls returned from the Pleiades. You are souls who are actively being taught in way-stations [6]in the constellations that hold the records of earth and all of its historical past. You are many and yet you are, as a group, one great and lighted being that has carved change in many ways.

We commissioned you to carry this work reaching many places of the planet, to interpret the work, to envision this work in pictorial form for those whose languages have difficulty in extracting these particular patterns of thinking. There is much that you can

------

[6] A place in spirit

assimilate and begin to bring into motion for the planet to enjoy in its consciousness expression.

Those who have foreseen the crises in its concentrated points fear for the change. They have their own directions. They serve their own purpose. **You are not to live in fear**, you are to live as minds transforming the negativity to its enlightened state. You are the visionaries to hold the patterns of the cosmic truth into physical connection.

Now, soul causal bodies infused with the rays of the Amethyst Light is changing. Feel your conflicts melting away. So be it.

When you are ready to return to the physical consciousness activate a pyramid of light.

Process

We direct and assimilate in and about you the frequencies of Gold, Silver, Pink and Amethyst in a pyramid of light. We direct all of you to enter this pyramid and all who are part of your life. Know there is nothing within you that is not understood by your soul. Let your turmoil come before you. Let your fears be recognized, and observe these as illusions of the unwise.

Once again, we cannot relay the time from which the completion of this process takes place. Individually you are assisted in your particular growth.

To close the session we see you are in thresholds of change, that pain changes, that fear changes, that resistance changes and all things as obstacles to your life are enveloped in divine love and achieving harmony. So it is.

We confirm all that is a part of you is balanced with light shielding your aura.

As your awareness moves back, when you awaken you will be in peace.

Lesson Twenty

COLOR RAY: MINT GREEN

The Light of Renewal and Rejuvenation

Message & Meditation #1

Into a State of Grace

We experience this energy uplifting and raising the frequency of the physical bodies and all consciousness from the tiniest cell to the largest organic structure within the body.

Once again, whatever fears exists holding you in abeyance to change and affects the organic and nervous systems of your physical nature, let the illusion of these fears be released. Wherever there is disorder or disharmony within the physical body, release it to the light.

Perceive the frequency of this light clearing away any sensitivities or psychic debris attached to your consciousness from past to present life activity. Focus on balance in the body and all levels of your multi-dimensional being. Whatever you think or feel mentally, physically and emotionally, ask destiny to come into wholeness in all dimensions as you walk the path of your individual realization.

The frequency of this light of the Radiant Mint Green feels like a healing energy moving throughout your physical body. Like a breath of new life, new consciousness it activates movement and change. As this energy rises through the body, perceive all systems, cellular, organic, glandular, reproductive, digestive, circulatory and respiratory, all enveloped in This Mint Ray.

Now rise up through the body and the Rainbow Bridge of Light into the inner planes and the level of the higher self where you greet your teachers and Masters,

Now move deep into the silence.

I am Brother Josiah. I speak so that you may hear with words of truth upon you as you exist in this presence of light.

Each of you have come through the path to this point in which your soul is turning away from all karmic activity of its own creation and moving forward into an extension of a higher level of its soul reality. The records have opened individually throughout this total level, or what you call a process. There have come moments in which your spiritual self has listened to the calling of the Council of Light to accept a new law upon your soul. This is the law in which grace of the higher self actively manifests internally throughout your whole life expression.

You have come upon a new plateau. You are no longer to think of self in a karmic wheel. You are no longer to see yourself as bonded to conditions unresolved. You are no longer to see yourself cloistered in ineffective experiences bound by the barriers and blockages of negative thinking.

You have all asked that the record be opened, that the way be made clear for you to hold yourself in a new light and to experience the energy of love as the source that brings self into the activity of grace. This is not to hold you individually into a self-aggrandizement where you become separated from all those who walk through the pathways of initiation.

Long before you were born, long before you remember being alive in the body, you were part of Mind. You were part of the many of this dimension of creativity; you were one of the beings of light. All that you see and all you create within the physical world has its beginning in light.   Within this Mind, your thought is a manifestation. Your ideas are an expression. Mind is like a garden where seeds are planted. The seeds develop and grow with thoughts, intentions and desires bringing them into full expression.

Mind is the garden of light and the garden of life. In Mind you are in this reality, in this place where all that you wish to see has its seed in consciousness. The records have been open for you to review and have been touched by Grace, the law of balance. Now in this state of mind you enter into this reality and all that you wish to see in life you live humanly has its beginning in this garden of light. You nurture your creativity and consciousness with the divine principles of love

So, frequencies of Mint Green bring to Mind the consciousness of creating, of creation, of new life, of beginnings formed as seeds within dimensions of light. Here you contemplate, and here you dream. In this state you exist as one of many, yet individually and conceptually, a perfect expression of God Creator/Father of all that is.

Perceive now, in this place all the seeds of all the ideas are planted in Mind and through your contemplation, through your rest, through your state of quietness, the vibration connects with you and all that is meant to be is a part of you.

This is the energy to dream with, to be in total silence, contemplation, restoration and recreation. It is within this dimension the process of your manifestation transpires.

Some of you are in need of restoring your body, the body you live in. Some of you need to restore your faith, your trust, your hope and your dreams. These are the moments of recreating and re-experiencing your own pattern innocently created from the origin of your being.

Many of you will receive insights of creation or of the many worlds in creation. Many of you see the beginning of planets and stars in space. Many of you will be curious in the history of earth and its beginning. Some of you will just be re-creating your consciousness in the physical world, seeing new Light, color and growth of it is of perfect intention and spiritual purpose. Some of you will have physical changes, changes of opportunities, new beginnings in your path, new lessons for all you wish to explore.

Some of you meet your Masters and teachers. Some of you see great beings of light. Some of you see the earth enveloped in many frequencies and some of you see that life in the earth has new opportunities.

As you hold this vision recognize you are participating in surrounding the earth and radiance in the frequencies for new life. Perceive the Mint Green Ray and the frequencies of its consciousness surrounding the planet. Perceive you are part of all the many of lighted ones magnifying this radiance.

The planet is a beautiful place in space. It is lush, green and varied in all its many life forms and life activity. However, the vibrations of humanity create dark clouds of confusion. See all mentally, emotionally and psychically clouded with confusion released from this consciousness. Visualize Earth enveloped with the light of new beginnings.

Doorways and gateways to higher planes are opening for many, receiving the influence, the impact; the connection to the Cosmic Christ is manifesting and elevating you to higher realities. You will travel in Mind to places seeing the greater need for the light. Changes taking place in governments, in leadership, in countries, and those under new regimes, new perspectives, perceive the light of Cosmic Consciousness healing them.

When you are ready, move back into the physical dimension.

Magnify a pyramid of light, Silver and Gold, Pink, Amethyst and Mint Green all magnified. As you center in this pyramid of energy, invite family, friends and others in the network of light to join you in this energy field of light. Feel your pyramid a place of gathering for restoring love and harmony connecting to a higher consciousness.

Whatever difficulties have played a role in the lessons, now it is just a wisp, a cloud swept into the light and cleared. You are one with each other and all part of the same dream. Each of you can become newly aware of all that you are.

When you are ready the radiance of Mint Green flows through you and all that has been given. Perceive it flow from the top of the head, down through the feet earthing your dream, your vision and your reality. Ground your dream, your visions through the Black Power Ray.

Lesson Twenty One

COLOR RAY: SCARLET

Passion

Message & Meditation #1

Inner and Outer Power and the Cosmic Activity

Activate the meditation procedure

As we move into the frequency of the Radiant Scarlet Energy, ask truth come into knowledge at a conscious level and all falseness be released. Affirm; destiny within the core of your own soul be fully activated, magnified and directed throughout all systems in the present.

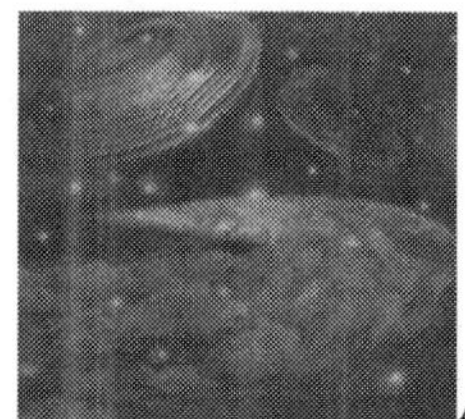**Artist Kathy Nadalin**

Rise up, experiencing your consciousness moving through the central vertical axis, through the Rainbow Bridge of Light, until you come into the temple where once again you meet with the Council of Light, the great, beautiful radiant ones that share in your personal evolution.

Message

I, Andrew, greet you in the light and the spirit of wisdom of your own being. I speak with you in the moment for you to hear with clarity that you in this precious moment in time are unfolding once again into a new form of self-image, a new perspective of your own ideal, a new directive of your own power and a new extension of your higher self. Think on these things.

You, in consciousness, have no perspective of the reality of your true power to create the will of the inner self to the outer plane. Limiting objectives of your outer life may hold you into a state of weakness, rather than extend into powerful demonstrations of your inner desire.

Through the vibration of this frequency, traumatic action occurs to unleash the hidden forces within your life. Release in this moment any thought you are weak, without self-direction and held back from your goals and dreams. Let go of thinking, feeling or denying your own wealth, fulfillment and joy based on conditions of outside sources. Release these illusions into the light. Perceive the flame of this energy directed in and through every perspective of you as an individual.

Do not fear, your own power use power wisely. The power of this Scarlet Ray will not to come fullness within until you claim your wholeness as absolute.

The frequency of this light is a base vibration stemming from the lower spine, the center of the creative nature of your own physical form. It is associated with the flow of the life force. Perceive Scarlet now actualized in consciousness within this inner dimension. See, feel and know the lighted body also is within the frequency of this ray.

You are the powerful and yet minute in your own perspective. The knowledge of this Scarlet Kundalini Fire energy magnifies to assist your physical body. To experience this Fire Energy in its fullest form requires clearing of any personal greed and self power. The

Kundalini Fire is experience in its full initiation as you progress into the next level of the lightwork. Your experience and integration of this becomes clear as you move in and through the levels and the initiation process within the next levels of the Lightwork.

For now, beloved students, focus on this light moving in the network of energy to block the explosions of powers misplaced, to block the rages and passions of distorted wills and to block the injustices of humanity's actions on behavioral systems. The power that will be unleashed to the earth through the cosmic rays and cosmic activity will be affecting each one. You who have processed the personal energies will find the frequencies conducive to action in a positive form.

There are many within the earth held imprisoned against the destinies of their own soul's designs. These are karmic experiences and causes coming into an effect out of alignment with the earth's unfoldment. You are in crucial moments of the earth's evolution. The powers that erupt in destructive energy and explode in human behavioral patterns, unleashed without discipline, cause blockages to the integration of spirit and Mind. Therefore, you are enveloped in this vibratory energy to learn of its inner reaction within every particle of your own being.

When you conquer this, you conquer much. This ray becomes a force that pleases the self and used in its highest manner.

When you come into a new expression of your own self-hood, what you then create becomes a blessing to many as well as to self. As karmic conditions are unleashed from you, as karmic conditions are resolved on the inner planes, you now become stewards of a new form of energy, which is the dynamic aspect of your individual self.

Your tests will come.

As the Master Christ received testing of His own Will by the powers and the principalities of the unknown, by temptations to rule the earth, so also are you presented with options that turn your head.

Discern as you grow, as you excel and as you integrate. As you expel the negatives, so shall it be, you will be free and you will have placed this energy in its highest perspective within you.

Each of you in this precious moment in time, feel the essence of this ray. Accept it as a challenge; bless it as a part of you, as a necessary part of your own physical desire systems. Perceive it balanced within all stages of your own self-knowing.

The earth must leash its power before it comes to the destructiveness of its own intent. The earth erupts and the coming times are to change many things. But do not fear, for as you walk with the guidance of your higher knowing, integrated with the reality you are a being of light, you are empowered.

Through this particular vibration, many things will come to your conscious knowing. Until that comes into effect, be yourself not in despair.

I, Andrew, overshadow you. Much of what I speak will not be held remembered, but as you awaken, the body will once again feel a new sense of its own physical form in power and strength.

Go in peace and may the light of the Christ be in and through you.

Notes

SECTION THREE

PLANETARY 9

THE KUNDALINI

INTRODUCTION

Greetings, this is Azreal.

I bring forward insight into the progress of walking the path of light. Every step taken is an opportunity to balance conditions within all levels of personal consciousness. Each and all are subject to the physical reality stimulating the conditions of both positive and negative forces. Each and all are awakened in the path of light to new abilities, insights and understanding within the body, mind and soul.

Entering into this stage of activating the Kundalini Fire energy is approaching the transformational phase of all physical conditions of one's own personal body, mind and spirit. The life force is the source that sustains all systems. The life force is the vibration, energy and consciousness connected to the base of one's spinal system. The chakra center magnified is from the center of the Scarlet Ray. The center itself is the source of stimulating the fire energy of Kundalini consciousness.

To be activated within the Kundalini system is to enter a readiness for the passion and desire of the true impulse of the Mind, the spirit and all that is connected to the higher reality of life.

Kundalini can bring into activation challenges regarding the use of power, regarding the use of intent and regarding the use of expectations of comparing your own self to what you see surrounding you and what others may create in their reality.

To be activated in Kundalini prior to any healing process, may result in loss of balance of reason, logic and right use of Will.

To be intensified within the Kundalini without the steps of preparation can result in outbursts of personality disorders or physical maladies. Therefore it is cautiously given. However, each and all of you who have entered the phase of this stage are in preparation, internally and externally to experience the magnificent light, the joy of being empowered to follow your higher self, the will of your inner knowing and the completions of interactions with your relationships in life.

Kundalini is a joyous journey when you surrender to accept the guidance of your own spirit and all who stand as guardians of your path.   Your experience with Kundalini Fire will vary.   Some of you will seem less touched in the process.   Others may find extreme intensities seeking to complete their life's needs.   Some of you will find you are impassioned with visions, hope and will to create what you came to complete in your soul's experience.

The affect of Kundalini is a state of being free from false intensions, from revenge and from all human behavior that would cause harm in another's way.   Those who experience the flow of Kundalini within all the systems of the body find they have elevated to a new phase of peace in readiness for the Angelic System.

Kundalini Fire initiation is not to be exempt from *the Course* or from *the path*.   It is an important part of the initiative aspect of your spiritual journey.   The Life Force is relative to what others may say as, " the soul or the heart of the matter."   Kundalini can be seen, felt or known inside of you as the burning desire to achieve, the impulse to overcome and as the status of moving past obstacles.   It seems to initiate inner strength and courage to pass through obstacles in the way.

Kundalini Fire is a positive part of the human nature.   It comprises the energy that stirs stagnation, unrevealed emotion and perception in need of being expressed.

Without the previous processes, it could bring great confusion and outbursts of behavior causing fear in others as well as within yourself.   But, beloved students, you are in the guidance and love of light of those who see and heal with love all that needs to be uncovered.

So to step into this phase is to graduate to a new plateau of personal wellness in human behavior, spiritual insight and spiritual action. Without passion, there is no action. Without intense direction, there is no manifestation. Kundalini assists in manifesting your hopes, your wishes and your dreams that unfold from the Mind of your higher self.

So, the fire aspect moves within the body and is associated with your spinal system. Your spinal cord and the spinal nature is the foundation of your physical consciousness, the structure that you stand with strength. When the spinal system is in weakness or in pain, there are many attributes associated with injury from past life, or injury from present time, or injury from the constant fear of being powerless against situations without freedom and love.

So, this is an awakening in your body, in your Mind, and in your soul to be free from all the ill winds of past pain and conditions. Kundalini Fire is felt often in sleep states as extreme heat that rises up your own spinal cord. There are moments when the warmth and heat is extremely intense. It can become almost an uncomfortable physical experience.

Some will see flashes of light as though you are rising out of the body and moving into dimensions far past what you perceived before. Others will feel numbness or extreme pain suddenly released and freed. The healing process within the Kundalini Fire is impressive for each and all who receive and surrender without fear and are open to growth.

Each of the processes within the meditations are guided by the Council and each of you are always within the thought, heart and soul of the lighted ones who guide you.

So accept this with an open mind, experience it with a fearless heart and enjoy it with the passion of love. Let go of resistance to being free from all your past negativity.

This stage is a welcome step leading through and into the Angelic Plane of higher consciousness. You will find great excitement, adventure and awakenings within your thoughts, emotional consciousness and your physical reality.

Walk in peace, always knowing you are exploring and growing, and so it is.

MEDITATION PROCEDURE

Meditation now is so comfortable you can perceive yourself energized as you direct thought into the forebrain.

Observe how your consciousness gathers all the egos and follows through with activating the centers of light in the Mercabah as in the Soul Body of Light.

As each center activates, with awareness rise up through the Rainbow Bridge to the level where you meet with the hierarchy. In the silence, experience your connection with the Council of Light. In this level of spirit, connect with the Network of Light for planetary healing. When you complete your planetary meditation, the integration of the Kundalini Fire process is directed by the Council of Light.

You will observe that the inner work taking place focuses on the Kundalini Fire connecting with all the centers of your physical body. The activation of the Kundalini is also imprinted within all centers of light. The activation of the Kundalini Fire energy spirals up the spinal cord. A powerful process occurs in which the desire of the highest self connects to your basic third dimensional self.

When you complete the inner work, ground your consciousness through the Black Power Ray.

Always close off your aura and magnetic field by moving the energy in a clockwise motion.

Lesson Twenty Two

COLOR RAY: WHITE

The Kundalini

"The greater the degree of self-realization, the
greater the need to be in that inner chamber of light
and in silence of one's own self."

Message & Meditation #1

We speak with each of you on a note to bring a new direction in personal consciousness, to prepare for upliftment and magnification of all the senses. We speak to release conditions within the lower selves that block your inner knowing of your true destiny.

We greet you with this thought. *You are going to experience within this round tremendous upliftment of your nature. You will enter a stage of consciousness where you **become free** from bondage denying the spiritual, mental and emotional compatibility of your life experience.* Trust and know things that now stand as blockage to your growth will be released and you will flow with these experiences.

The activities of the past brought you to a point where you feel and know your own sensitivity. Still you may feel certain frustrations within yourself.

Let go of fears and anxieties denying your personality its control. In this time and place, each of you are free from any expression that would hold you in a state of negativity. Understand you are moving in a multi-dimensional way through a quickened evolution in this particular incarnation. There are many steps to transmute the lower forces into a higher state of being.

Many of you have experienced changes in the way you perceive your own consciousness by the changes in desires of where you focus your energy. Know there are yet many stages to move through before you truly know and understand the envelopment of love that must be the expression of all of your being.

Therefore, the direction for the following cycle will be to bring forth new miracles of your growth. The miracle of healing, of light and of love is contained within the seat of your own consciousness. Daily communication within this inner chamber is the key opening the door to inner knowing beyond the grasp of one's own self.

The growth of your individual selves is beyond measure by your conscious mind. You cannot measure that expansiveness, you can only see reflections of your growth by those who seek your own counsel and come to you to learn. You can only judge the need for your own growth by those from whom you absorb a greater teaching.

Resistances sometimes occur at the level of the conscious mind when there are imageries that it cannot move beyond its own dissension. If dissension magnifies, release it to the light. Know all dissenting factors are imageries and created perceptions.

This particular cycle is a very intense cycle. Know it will not interfere with performing the duties of your everyday experience. As the integration of the Kundalini Fire energy comes into action, you are further freeing yourself.

Each center of the Soul body of Light integrates with the physical body and astral/etheric with the Kundalini Fire. Each time you have a new dimension to work through, there are clearings that take place.

Physical obstacles appear and conscious thoughts can deny the right action of activity unless you perceive these obstacles and conflicts resolved through higher laws of love. All is in right thought and right expression when given through the laws of love and through the spirit of the Christ.

To receive the consciousness of love, you must perceive yourself as a reflection of your compassion. When you are able to let go of all conditions disturbing you and center in your own space, mind and indwelling self, you know the "peace that passes all understanding." Peace is the light that surrounds you as a protecting shield. Your magnetic and dynamic fields are a reflection of your thoughts, emotions and spiritual consciousness.

As you move through the planetary stages, activating the pyramidal structures, the vibrations become more clarified and more magnified. The centering becomes more applicable in everyday experience. *"It is within the inner chamber, in the temple of one's own being and in the silence of that temple, one receives the inner knowing and the keys to the Kingdom of Light. This kingdom dwells in and about your individual being."*

Silence is the greatest asset to your spiritual growth. It is within the silence you know, hear, see, feel, express, expand and anticipate the door opening consciousness beyond human reality. The greater the degree of self-unfoldment, the greater the need for the inner light and the silence of one's own self.

Meditation Process

The presence of your higher self brings upliftment and unifies all egos into one consciousness as they rise up into the center of the Radiant White Light. The star bursts forth in fullness, moving into a sphere, surrounding the mental body and all thought that exists from the conscious self and the unconscious.

Affirm all thoughts that resist accepting the purity of light now released.   Perceive its vibration moving in and through the physical body where all the attributes respond to this energy to cleanse and clear. Purification is the goal, along with clarity.

Perceive the energy moving in and through the emotional body. Let the feelings that lie in this level be raised up by the energy of the Radiant White Light. See this energy now moving through the perceptual body. Whatever psychic attachments exist perceive them released into the vibration of energy. The cellular, organic and all the physical nature is raised in the vibration of this light.

As this essence magnifies, perceive it activated in and through the mental, emotional, perceptual and physical bodies.

Follow the meditation procedure.

Perceive your higher self within this inner chamber open for new awareness and experience new joy and opportunities for service. Through service, you attain that consciousness of being a part of all you encounter. See yourself becoming more united in consciousness with those who are enveloped in the patterns of growth and self-expression.

In this inner chamber of light, feel the presence of the teacher of your own being and the guides of your own consciousness. Be still. Let the body be relaxed and let the mind be totally in touch with its own expressions.

As you center within this radiant essence of the White Light, perceive it now moving throughout the networking of energy that surrounds the earth planet. Flow with mind and consciousness and the activity of the Council of Light.

Perceive yourself moving through the experience connecting with the network of light, the bands of energy surrounding the planet earth and directing the rays of purity, clarity and cleansing as though the earth star becomes encompassed with the power of the light to bring into reality that which aligns the body to the spirit and the mind to the soul.

Visualize all human beings raised in their own self-evolution to the point of knowing the nature of truth and love. Perceive the impurities, the abominations, the destruction, and the conditions in opposition to the inner peace released to the light. Perceive the thoughts dissipating the mental syndromes of apathy and of despair. Perceive movement as causes raising the level of life for all humanity, the karmicly bound as well as those who have attained levels of grace.

It is very difficult to see the earth in a position of cleansing, but you must in Mind perceive the earth as a pure radiant star, cleansed of all its polluted activities and impurities. The more minds that can magnify the perfection of the earth's activity, the greater can be the influx of the cosmic spirit through all levels of its being.

Bring your energies, thoughts and consciousness back to the soul center of your own vibration and activate the essence of the White Light in a pyramidal structure. Perceive selves completely enveloped in the activity of the five-sided White pyramid.

The purpose of being centered in these pyramidal vibrations is to help create a place for total self-containment and self-release, to help clear and cleanse what is within and without, and to act as a source of magnification of the energy frequencies.

Call forth the loved ones of your own consciousness, those who are close to the heart and to your experiences. Bring them into the light. Let go of conditions that cause pain to your mind and to your heart. Release those within the systems of personality that have no part to play in future expression. Free yourself from the negativity and dissension and see the pure purpose of relations and relating. Feel the joy of the love within self.

In your outer, daily lives it is important to take time to love yourself and your total expression. Oftentimes, your own beingness is a stranger to the conscious self and there arise the embattlements between this conscious self and who you are physically. Love this physical self and love your body. As you love the body, it will begin to react, as you love it to be

Now move to the core of your own centered self or soul desire.

In the past cycle, much karmic entanglement was dissipated by reviewing the encounters of your established selves in different frameworks of life. You were processing and breaking the codes of creative thought within karmic entanglements of life. Within this center, we now move to the core of your own centered self or soul desire.

The power of desire is to know itself as an absolute creative center in which it experiences completion of its full pathway to wholeness. Your soul's desire is multi-faceted as you are unique in your simplicity and complexities.

So, in this present moment, soul becomes enveloped in rays of light and magnified in frequencies that are associated with the power of itself—the life force. It is the energy stemming from the lower aspect of the body, the Scarlet Ray. From that center, the vibration is brought into a magnified expression.

Release in the now all fear that this center itself is the cause of your downfall, causing you to feel you are lesser than meant to be. Let go of imageries that power, the force of your desire, is a negative element. Let go the fear that the power within this center should be avoided.

Perceive in the moment that this vibration of light travels throughout the physical body, throughout all the astral / etheric plane and is in direct connection to the soul body. Perceive also the causal desire of the soul, implanted in its own memory, becoming enveloped in the Scarlet Ray of light. Accept you are experiencing this merging to unleash the reality of your completed selves.

And now, each of you will begin to feel the vibrant flow attuning itself to the inner consciousness as you go deep, deep into the inner chamber of your being and merge with the flame of energy and light. Meditate, beloved students, on self emerging into the marriage of your higher being. The gift of the experience will be revealed to you in the inner heart.

Your lessons will be in communicative skills, in the objective, assertive experiences of your egos, and in the way you entangle your nature in causes without wisdom. The outcome should bring you where you are free from the fear of oppression, persecution, illusion, deceit, weakness, timidity, hostility and rage.

Dwell on the thought that you are love and you love in all things that live and move and have their being. You are one with life and life lives through you. You encompass life as though you patterned it in a unique tapestry of your own design. When you are in harmony with your creation, then your creation is the pattern of the image of the level of Christ.

Go in peace now, beloved ones, and walk with strength and wisdom.

Lesson Twenty Three

COLOR RAY: GOLD

Transmutive

"In this planetary center is the dimension of the
first creation. It incorporates the beginning
stages—the creation of other creators. The earth
can only be uplifted through the transmutation and
cleansing of the Planetary Mind."

Message

There is some confusion within thoughts regarding the dimension
of the higher self or the planetary vibration. We desire to bring
these thoughts into a clearer vision of yourself as you exist in all of
the planes and dimensions.

The planetary center is one aspect of your higher dimensional
being. Through the planetary self, you can walk through the doors
of yet other planes of knowledge. It is through the planetary
consciousness, which is an element of spirit that you break through
the closed doors to yet other realities of Cosmic Sense and
universal knowledge. Within the planetary center, you have the
key to open up the way to understand the elements of science or
the philosophy. All truth, all thought and all wisdom exist within
this level of spirit.

It is difficult in your minuteness to understand the linkage of self
to a grander scale of the macro element. You cannot focus within
the conscious self and understand the immensity of the macro
expression—the earth image in its greater potential. You have
glimpses of this reality by seeing things in an ideal state of
thought. You have glimpses of what you know as perfection from

ideas of your own creation, but you cannot encompass all that truly is at the macro level.

In the planetary level, the work of light begins to help transmute all forms of self, as well as mass-mind activity. It is through this plateau of consciousness where the service of light moves to connect with all the networks of other activities.

Beyond the planetary being is yet the angelic activity. Once one unifies their own selves with the planetary vibration, there can be a moving on into yet a higher level of the angelic selves. But through this cycle, there still must be the inner cleansing in and throughout the lower forms and a greater integration of the planetary self.

Therefore, each of you is being enveloped in consciousness of the planetary element. And as this takes place the frequencies of light are magnified throughout all of the lower planes to begin the healing and the dissipation of conflicts that are still present within your physical being.

Through past experience on the path of light, you have become more acquainted with the elements of your own physical being. You moved with awareness into the soul's activity. You perceived your soul as a radiant essence of frequency and light, color, Mind and experiences from all elements of expression. The desire of the soul is to free itself and to fulfill itself creatively, spiritually, mentally and physically.

You have been told that the physical plane must come into balance and harmony with the inner soul. As this transpires and the union becomes a reality on all levels, there is a sense of rising above many lower elements and yet walking amongst each aspect with an inner peace and a sense of movement to heal. As the soul expands and becomes more magnified, it releases the impurities within its own being and begins to bridge the activity to the higher self, you rise up into that being of your own individual spirit.

It is most important to manifest within your nature a total perception of being in right thought with the consciousness of the Christ to assimilate the teachings of His vibration as manifested through the life of Jesus. This is to know that through the works of love and through the works of service comes the upliftment of your own inner being.

Through the giving of consciousness to those who are ready to receive the inner planes of light, there is reward. Know that through change of your own expression comes an upliftment of your outer body. Perceive the body as an instrument and a vehicle for love and for the purpose of bringing into action the works of the Christ Consciousness.

The vibration of the Cosmic Father is the element to work through in this present time and activity. The radiant essence of the Golden Ray is the vibratory sounds that raise all frequencies. It is still beyond all conscious knowing to understand the true process, but the vibrations of your conscious mind is tuning into the experiences of moving throughout the inner planes and connecting with the vibrations of the higher beings. Begin to perceive your planetary consciousness as an embodiment in spirit of mind, knowledge, wisdom and truth. Think, be and flow in this radiant essence of light.

The conscious mind may question, *"What is the purpose? What is the result? What is the effect?"* The effect is many minds becoming as one vibration, a tremendous sound of light that breaks through the mental barriers of lower conditional thought. All opposition to the spirit of truth, to peace, to love and to harmony is dissenting or discordant consciousness.

Perceive now your Mind as one vibration magnified and part of yet greater beings of light. Perceive this as a moving force in and throughout the planetary consciousness of all spirits. Perceive a transformation of all polluted, conditional thought activity. Again, one is in total integration when one flows through the processes with internal and external light and love of all being and all entities.

In this planetary center is the dimension of the first creation. It incorporates the beginning stages, the creation of other creators. The earth can only be uplifted through the transmutation and cleansing of the planetary mind. Through all ages the hierarchy has worked with you and lifted up their total selves into this plane of being to help the unfoldment and evolution of conditions that are in opposition to the greater good. More energy is needed to dissipate the activities that are of destructive forces.

Events to come are transmuted through the power of thought, through the power of Mind and through the vision of perfection that comes through those who desire to see a new plane of expression. The service of light is the greatest purpose both individually and collectively. You, as light workers, are tuning into the sounds and vibrations to uplift all systems.

All in all, we perceive many changes have come into focus. Each change will have its own source of consciousness. We perceive that the work must be intensified and brought into a clearing, focusing on the actualization of the spirit through the egos of personality systems.

Every being must understand that he is in total activity of his own consciousness and must assimilate as to purpose and desire. Know that through knowledge and understanding of self, there is a sense of consciousness that brings things into a greater experience of realization.

Wisdom comes from beyond knowledge, from the elements of spirit and sees itself as uplifters of all physical planes. Therefore, ask that knowledge and wisdom come into focus and integrate within your inner being as well as your conscious self.

The key phase to this cycle is to integrate at all levels the higher knowing. It is to experience the divine love within your spirit and within your lower consciousness. It is to love unconditionally all of your creation.

What appears as unlovable is an image of distortion. Think of it in its true perfected state, for this is the key to transmutation. You perceive things as one developed state, but your inner self bypasses the outer distortions and sees it as perfect and whole. The miracles occur through transmutation. What you desire to express creatively, accept as already in fullness as you move towards that goal or expression.

Let go of conditional thought, limited by its own perception. Sense the greater whole. Perceive self-objectifying the creative nature in a positive direction, flowing with the laws of spirit and the laws of mind.

The Age of Aquarius as in this Millennium dawns with a New Hope. While you have perceived and been given the heavier events to take place, keep in mind that there is also the greater good which is going to be manifested.

The healing arts will bring forth new miracles to help recreate and regenerate the cells and limbs. There will be discoveries that will come forth to alleviate much of the diseases that are today so prevalent within the organic systems. Perceive the healing flowing through all consciousness.

As you work in Mind you are increasing the vibration of bringing forth the greater good into the earth plane. Perceive the political structures within the nations letting go of the dissension and ancient karmic ties. See the earth being balanced through the cosmic element and brought to a point of awakening.

Perceive all knowledge as a facet for understanding the elements, the life experiences, and the activities of human consciousness. Perceive all knowledge as a way to bring things into a greater understanding within the intellect. It is simply a tool.

The wisdom of the higher self far surpasses the knowledge gained and comes as a descending light that brings about an inner peace through the releasing of past conditioning and negations. Affirm the Will of the Father manifesting through the Son of your own consciousness and into the physical.

Ask and it shall be given, **but you may not know the time of its fulfillment.** Be in faith that you may be freed from the limitations of your own awareness. Faith brings to self a sense of rising above conditions as they exist on the outer planes, faith in accepting the inner light and power of the highest self, that which is aligned to the spirit, to the mind and to the laws of the higher consciousness, moving through all activities. Know that your elder brother (masters) has walked each step along your path. Your elder selves have joyously experienced each accomplishment. And now, be at peace. May the light of the Christ be in and through you.

Meditation Process

With your consciousness focused in light, perceive all egos gathered, uplifted by the centers and consciousness of the higher self. Rise with all the egos unified in one consciousness into the center of the Radiant White Light. Once again, experience the vibration of this energy magnified and directed into a sphere moving in a counter-clockwise motion. Release the thoughts within the mental level that are negative, fearful and reductive. Perceive this Radiant White Light clearing the aura and releasing conditioned thought patterns.

Now perceive this light moving in and through the emotional body. Release all the feelings that lie within the consciousness of this emotional nature that deny your self-acceptance. Perceive the Radiant White Light moving in and through the perceptual body. Ask that whatever psychic debris has been absorbed, collected, attached or created be released in this flame of energy.

Once again, activate the crown chakra, the energy of the Golden Light, perceiving this frequency magnified. Experience yourself enveloped within this ray of energy until it surrounds you centered within this light.

In the center of the Radiant Blue ray activate this vibration. All mental anger, repressed feelings, thoughts, confusion, conflict, and rage, release into the energy of the Radiant Blue ray. See doubts about yourself, about life, change, things unknown, see them all consumed in the radiance of energy. Perceive the flow of this light moving into the all of the cellular system and the organic nature until the body is completely infiltrated with wisdom and self-knowing.

Now move into the throat chakra and feel the essence of this Emerald Ray moving into the magnetic field. If there are any experiences of being suppressed or overly magnetic, absorbing too much or being bottled up, perceive the Emerald Light moving in and through the consciousness of the subjective self. Direct the energy into the dynamic vibration, once again affirming your motivation, your desire and your creative intent. Perceive that your actions are in balance and harmony with all experiences. Clear sadness, pain and confusion and release all psychic impressions that leaves an imprint in your consciousness.

Experience all the chakras open and clearing your body.

Rise with awareness up through the central vertical axis, through the Silver Chalice, upward in consciousness into the planetary center where you greet the teachers, guides, counselors, and masters.

In the process of your developed self coming to its state of joy and wholeness, you explore the adventures of where you have been. You perceive what lies in future time through impressed energies from the vast resources of the universal mind.

You have all experienced exposures to what is called the mental patterns of prophetic action through insights and directives of outside sources. The prophecies given to you have their bearing on the outcome of the earth's experience through its purifying state. But as the teachers of your soul through the mental transmutative consciousness, we direct you to let go of the harbored anxieties and reflections of chaotic changes in the earth expression.

Visualize in the moment that you, as a part of Mind of the greater whole, direct the transmutative Golden Ray into the earth's expression, as though the earth is encompassed in all you see as light. Know that what appears as devastation is lifted from the imageries of man, the imageries of the astral forces and from the imageries of the ancient prophecies. Visualize cosmic rays integrating with human souls bringing about the internal awakening to an external choice of positive action.

Again, as the earth enters into the cycle of its accelerated growth, there are many karmic bonds that cling to the collective energy. To bring release to the karmic bonds, it is important that the minds of men and all that inhabit the earth, experience higher cosmic rays of light. As we work internally within you to empower the desire systems of your individualized soul, you become a reflective mirror of the positive forces of light and love.

Therefore, in this moment, perceive that the flame of light of the Kundalini Fire within the center of your soul desire is activated, empowering the desire of self to focus only on what brings healing into consciousness.

In this moment, perceive the soul of self and the desire / causal nature enveloped in the flame of light in the hues of the Scarlet Ray. Perceive the power of this desire merging with a network of energy bringing into action a cosmic event of light, a lifting of the human self into its higher cosmic expression. In your inner states of silence, accept the power of this light.

Few have experienced the full awakening of the light as the serpent through the spinal system to the soul. But as this is inflamed within you, fear not. Only know that your desire must have its complete and fulfilled expression. Internal and external changes will come into focus within the physical.

Lesson Twenty Four

COLOR RAY: BLUE

Wisdom

"Wisdom comes as a fleeting vibration of
awakening to an inner peace that transmutes all
fear and anxiety."

Message

This is Annanius and I see you in light, wisdom and in truth. I come to prepare you for the process in which you experience the further integration connecting you to the soul desire unfolding the action of your own individual nature into an integrated state with the power of your truth.

Individually, you experience intensities of light traveling in and through the multi-dimensional self from the planetary system of the Mind, through the soul and causal part of soul, through the astral and into the physical where the life force, based in the spine of your body, begins to flow upward as it is enlightened by the spirit and the sword of wisdom.

Multi-dimensional activity never can fully be comprehended by an intellectual nature. It can only be experiential through your individual experience. To language the process is almost foolish. However, in the presence of this activity find within yourself the awareness of power at the base of the spine and affirm this power be fully actualized and motivated by the absolute perfect divinity of your soul encounter with earth consciousness. Affirm that the power you are, is the power of love, fully realized in mental states of conscious thought.

Power must be visualized not as a sword to annihilate, not as a sword to produce negations in the evolving consciousness of another, not to act in a form that deviates the level of peace, but as a source that transmutes all fear. Power must be a realized energy that walks in its quietness, but in strength; a knowing, but direct, objective and constructive reasoning spirited by the Law of Love. The dragon (symbolic of the Kundalini Fire) lies asleep at the base until it is awakened. The fires begin to clear the crystallized states resistant to itself, spirit and light.

The message and key for this week's progression into higher states of initiation is to integrate the cosmic knowing that the divine will of the hierarchy is ever moving through all stages of creation. Know that your spirit and your individualized self is a connecting cord to the higher beings. Regardless of the obstacles of your pathway, you are still moving towards a total expression of a whole, true, unified being.

Meditation Process

We speak to you with love and joy and with a feeling of moving with your thoughts and awareness into a higher plane of experience. Enter into the Temple of Light. At this moment, put aside any physical distractions or any conscious thoughts of imbalance.

When you gather your awareness into the temple of the higher planes, you truly rise in consciousness to another level of experience. The masters and teachers merge with you bringing the energy of the Wisdom Ray into greater magnification within your own consciousness.

As you are in the temple, move with the frequencies of the Radiant Wisdom Ray to break through mental barriers of fear and doubt blinded to the truth. Rise up into the state of consciousness where you blend your vibrations with the activity of the lighted ones, moving in the vibration of the light of wisdom. Feel yourself connecting to a strong frequency and sound that breaks through the syndromes of fear, anger, rage and actions of opposing forces to the higher truth.

As you magnify this activity and frequency, begin to see yourself merging with all who are descending into this particular plane to help create the impact of upliftment upon the human thought and human mind. As you journey in and throughout this vibration to help uplift the earth consciousness, you are still working through your own individual journey. You are still breaking through the fears and doubts existing within your own thoughts.

Once again, we are going to bring into consciousness the activity of the causal aspect of your own soul consciousness. Focus on this aspect and know that to release within yourself the desires of your inner nature and to free the soul from its karmic activities within the earth is a very intensified process.

As we have accepted you within this system to initiate the acceleration of your own individual consciousness, you are now experiencing the intensity and the vibration. You are moving before the lords of karma, before those who have instigated your birth cycle into the earth expression. Again, intellect may not understand all that is transpiring, but perceive yourself within the inner Temple of Light releasing any remaining causal factors and imageries that would stand as a deterrent to the soul's progression and its true state of grace. Bring them before the lords of light and karma.

The essence of the Radiant Wisdom Ray is now moving through the total soul plane. Perceive the ancient fears, superstitions and denials being brought before these entities of light, who oversee karmic patterns. Perceive these karmic patterns being released from the soul system. Perceive a radiant laser light of blue cutting through the bonds that have entangled you to karmic patterns.

Ask that the crown of wisdom be placed upon the soul body to discern between truth and imageries of falseness. Seek in the silence the peace that passes all understanding. Let the tongues be silent before those who cannot know and let the ears be closed to those who ramble without direction. Again, wisdom comes as a fleeting vibration of awakening to an inner peace that transmutes all fear and anxiety. Release all arrogance and pride that comes from the conscious self unawakened to the inner truth and radiance of its source.

Affirm that you be brought into complete freedom from pain, anger and suffering from past to present conditioning. Affirm that the joy of light and the spirit of love move throughout your being. Know that to love is to experience self as another's vibration. See yourself within all consciousness, all entities and all beings. To see your inner self and all that you are reflected in those who are part of your expression in earth, be it great or small; is to know you are all as one. You cannot be divided and be in awakening of the spirit of truth, wisdom and love.

Now move through the networking of light, moving in the radiant sound and light of this frequency of Blue. Concentrate on the tremendous fears that motivate much of the activity in the masses of thought. Enslaved minds are those minds propagated by fear, anxiety and instability.

When one becomes centered and focused in that inner wisdom, one rises above the need to fear those who appear as the authoritative aspect. You blend with their being, equalized through the inner self. You may not know technologies or analogies of equal nature, but your true spirit is an equalized vibration, a divine spark out of the mind of the Creator. Perceive the divine nature coming to the forefront of all activities through the will of the highest selves.

When you have completed your journey, move back into your own center and let go of all conditions that would hold you in states of abeyance. It is good for you to be a part of this work of light. It is difficult at times. You feel discouraged by your own insensitivities and by a lack of awareness of the impact of what is truly transpiring. It is difficult to maintain a sense of uplifted understanding when the material plane is filled with many trials.

Again, know that your creations are as you have directed them to be. The lessons are great. Those who receive them with the knowledge and consciousness of the higher realms will integrate and incorporate and express that higher nature of knowing.

Begin to move through your Rainbow Bridge into the center of the Radiant Silver Ray and fill the magnetic field of your own consciousness with the essence of this light. Begin again the creation of a pyramidal structure of energy. These pyramid activities are most important to rise with consciousness to transmute, uplift and harmonize. The magnified energy is much stronger than your first awakening of the centers of light.

One must move through these progressions in a step-by-step process. Blend the essence of the Gold Energy into the dynamic side and the Radiant White Light into the backside of the magnetic field. You are now in this essence of energy. Create the vibrant Wisdom Ray as the front of the pyramid and fill the center with the

Radiant Blue, the base and the front. This will create a very strong, protective, vibrant pyramid to transmute, nourish, cleanse and to protect against fear.

Call forth those who are very much a part of your everyday experience, those who feel lost and separated from their own higher being. Call their souls into this vibration. All of the loved ones of your being ask the higher selves to bring them into this frequency. Each of you, individually, must make peace with self and all. Simply experience this as a communion of all of these beings of light.

Peace is with you and may the light of the Christ be present in all of your experiences.

Lesson Twenty Five

COLOR RAY: EMERALD GREEN

Creativity

"There are still many areas of expansion that lie before you. No matter how evolved a state one may attain, one is still subject to yet other expanding vibrations."

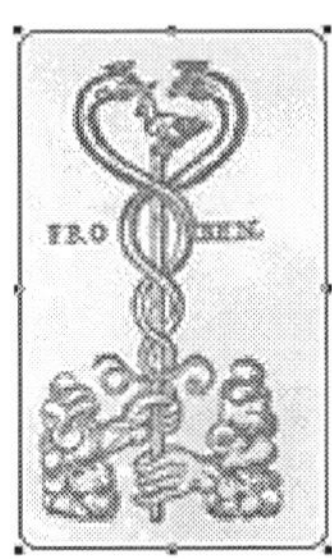

The word Kundalini is derived from a Sanskrit word *Kundal* meaning coiled up. It is the primordial dormant energy present in three-and-a-half coils at the base of the spine in a triangular bone called the Sacrum. The Latin name *Os Sacrum* suggests it is a holy or sacred part of the body. The ancient Greeks were aware of this and therefore they called it the *Hereon Osteon* noting that it was the last bone to be destroyed when the body is burnt and also attributed supernatural powers to it. Egyptians also held this bone to be very valuable and considered it the seat of special power.

In the West, Sacrum is symbolized by the sign of Aquarius and by the Holy Grail, container of the water of life.

The Kundalini, which is to nourish the *tree of life* within us, is coiled up like a serpent and, therefore, it has been called, *The Serpent Power*. It has been described in great detail in the Upanishads. Kundalini Yoga is supposed to be supreme in all the Yogas. Guru Vashistha asserted that Kundalini is the seat of absolute knowledge. The awareness of the presence of this primordial energy, Kundalini, within the human body was considered by the sages and saints to be the highest knowledge. The Kundalini and Chakras are vividly described in Vedic and Tantric texts.

In the Holy Koran

Prophet Mohammed Sahib talked of the day of resurrection when he says that the, *"hands will speak, that day we set a seal on their mouths, but their hands will speak to us, and their hands bear witness to all that they did."* When Kundalini awakening occurs, a flow of energy in the form of cool vibrations from the hands is experienced and the various Chakras felt on parts of the hand and fingers.

In the West

Christians called it "a reflection of the Holy Ghost," and worshipped its manifestations as tongues of flames over the heads of apostles during the Pentecost reunion.

Moses

Moses saw it in the form of the burning bush. During the exodus the Israelites lost faith and were smitten by fiery serpents so God told Moses *"Make thee a serpent, and set it upon a pole: and it shall come to pass, that everyone that is bitten, when he looketh upon it, shall live. And Moses made a serpent of brass and put it on a pole, and it came to pass, that if a fiery serpent had bitten any man, when he beheld the serpent of brass, he lived,"* An apt description of the healing qualities of the awakened Kundalini. Some of the Israelites even began to worship this symbol, and the practice of worshipping the brazen serpent on the pole as a god was either passed on, or was revived later. Bronze and stone serpent artifacts have been found in excavations in Canaan, Gezer and other parts of Israel!

Jesus Christ

The Old Testament symbol becomes significant in Christianity when Moses suggests Kundalini awakening, not just for the tribe of Israel but as the true destiny of all Christians: *"And as Moses lifted up the serpent in the wilderness, even as The Son f Man be lifted up that whosoever believeth in him should not perish but have eternal life"*

Tao

In the Tao Te Ching, the primordial power is described as that of a mother. Lao Tze described Kundalini as the *"spirit of the valley."* The spirit of the valley never dies. The spiritual instrument within us can be described as a microcosm (miniature form of creation) which links us to the Divine. The ancient esoteric text, "Scripture of the Golden Flower" also speaks of the effects of the awakened Kundalini energy.

Buddhist

The Lord Buddha spoke of the *"middle path"* to achieve Nirvana. He was actually describing the central channel (sushumna) through which the Kundalini ascends. Later Buddhist masters considered that the existence of the path of liberation within a human being was the greatest secret. They transmitted it to only a few deserving disciples.

Other Cultures

One also finds symbols of Kundalini in many different cultural legacies, such as Mercury's serpent, which is an alchemical symbol for the process of psychic metamorphosis. The Gnostics understood the serpent to represent the spinal cord. In ancient Greek and later, Roman mythology, we find Asclepius, the god of healing. He is seen holding a staff, which is entwined with a serpent (or sometimes two). Why did the Greeks relate this symbol to healing? The staff represents the central support of the human body or spinal cord (physical location of the *sushumna*. In Rome Aescaluius came to represent Mercury who usually held a healing staff called the Caduceus. The one or two coiled snakes or serpents entwined around the staff, represents the Kundalini, which rises along the central subtle channel in a spiral double helical movement.

Summary

The Kundalini is there to nourish, to heal and look after and to give an individual a higher and deeper personality. The power of Kundalini is absolute purity, auspiciousness, chastity, self respect, pure love, detachment, concern for others and enlightened attention, to give infinite joy and peace to an individual. [7]

Meditation

We speak with the light of your own higher selves. We bring into motion the egos of your own consciousness. Aligning them into

---

[7] http//www.soolcom.au/koe/14-02.htm

the forebrain, perceive all egos coming into mergence with the presence of the higher self. Uplifting and forming a vibration allows the egos to come into harmony, into balance and into a love expression where there is a total acceptance of each aspect of your consciousness.

Again, to come into alignment, one must let go of the scattered forces that stem from the stimulus of the physical plane and deter them from the actuality of the true higher nature. Discernment in perceiving where your energies are directed is most important at this point. Each of you understand that you are coming into a level where your word becomes a vibration that effects all who are a part of your experience and what you set forth can create an instant cause and effect activity.

While you have brought forth releases within the soul causal system and have moved into a new Law of Grace, you are still in response to the Law of Cause and Effect, but on a more activated and instantaneous consciousness. Therefore, be cautious where you project your thought and what you put into motion from individual consciousness.

Now let go of all heaviness within the physical plane, let go of all heaviness within the mental, emotional and perceptual. Let go of any sense of being caught in the webs of negation. Perceive the centers of light being activated and magnified.

In this session, we work with the Radiant Emerald Green frequency. As the energy comes into focus, release any form of being without activity to express your own creative consciousness. This is a time period where the creative self is desiring to come more into focus in a manner in which it communicates the intensity of the purpose of light and the purpose of gathering up all of the many different facets of its life's work.

As this frequency moves through the body, perceive all perceptions of yourself having a clear image, releasing all false-to-fact imageries regarding your own causal factors and releasing all projections of what you perceive others are activating or putting into motion. Discernment is the key to expansion and awareness. All of you are experiencing a heightened sensitivity within your feeling nature.

Release in this moment, any angers within the systems of the physical and direct the light to the organs for clearing the heavier, denser psychic forms.

Once more experience through your own systems, the purifying and the cleansing of imageries that would deny you a sense of being in completeness. Release the anger rages from past conditioning to present thought and perceive all of the physical aspects, the magnetic and dynamic selves, receiving the radiant energy to bring things into a total balance.

Know that you are very much an effect as well as a cause. But understand that you are lifting self into an even finer essence. You are, as you desire to be only to the degree that you understand the nature of your own energy and love vibration. The love essence must be the total core of your overall expression. Without the love element, you become without a sense of pure upliftment. Think on these things.

Perceive the essence of the Emerald Ray releasing fear and anxiety, usurping your own power system. You cannot be usurped of your power when you stay focused in the light, although you can drain others through your own misdirection of thought and energy. Therefore, be cautious and know that the light is an essence, a vibration of your inner consciousness. It must be utilized in its highest form for clearing and raising the activities that are now coming into focus through planetary consciousness.

The mass-mind element sees things from a state of fear and many who are a part of your everyday circle are experiencing the tremors of consciousness within their own being. You will stand as a symbol of peace, a symbol of integrity and a symbol of openness to higher mind and the principles of truth.

Once more you come into the Temple of Light and into the record of your soul's activity. Once more, perceive certain aspects of your soul's nature repeating patterns and conditioned to effects in contradiction to the inner spirit. Ask that these now come into awareness of intent. See them brought into balance interpersonally with all relations. Again, this must come in the inner silence and from your asking that you receive what is directly appropriate for your knowledge and understanding. Ask to see that which brings you into negative factors and which is now needed to be removed from your life that creates the disturbances and the upheavals.

There are still many areas of expansion that lie before you. No matter how evolved a state one may attain, one is still subject to yet other expanding vibrations. Feel yourself strengthened and cleared and yet, still within the continuing process of initiatory growth. There is much work yet to come that is beyond what the conscious mind can perceive at this moment. Therefore, it would be of great benefit for each of you to review certain aspects of *Revelations* (P4) and the interpretations given through the lesson materials, to review once more what the oversoul says to the consciousness as it works through the mind cells and through the consciousness of each center within your being. Review these once again to reacquaint yourself with what is transpiring as you cleanse these elements from within self.

Now the essence of the Emerald Green Ray moves in and throughout all aspects of your consciousness. Perceive the swords of light breaking through the clouds of doubt that would overshadow and deny your sense of being in tune with the intent of your higher will. You have all experienced much within these inner planes of activity and have risen through certain areas of higher awareness.

You have been told that you are freed from certain karmic causes, and yet, this does not mean that you will not be a part of other karmic activity. Understand that many come into your life who are attached from past relations, but you will feel less of a pull to be part of their karmic causes and will feel a greater sense of being a creator of creating new experiences.

It is not for you to feel a sense of superiority or a sense of being above another as this brings into motion new cause and effect activity. Simply perceive that you have released the need to become entangled in the dramas of their creation.

Move with your awareness through the networking of light that surrounds the earth and its entire aura. Visualize and perceive this planet as enveloped in the Radiant Emerald Green frequency. The earth is not an expression of lack; it is a whole, complete, abundant creation of its Creator. See this within the inner mind and know that it is a reality at this dimensional level. The earth itself seeks to come into its state of grace, therefore, the eruptions of karmic causes long held within its systems comes to the surface. This too shall pass.

See the light breaking the cords that have bound the earth in darkness. Perceive the planet and all who dwell upon it as one unified vibration, as an entity that is releasing its repetitive karmic patterns and is truly creating a new cycle of activity fulfilling the vision of what has been projected.

As you move through these inner dimensions when you are ready, bring your awareness back into your own planetary center and back into the centers of the soul.

Activate once again the structures of the pyramidal vibrations. Invite all you seek harmony, peace and healing to occur. As they are drawn into your pyramid, hold them in silence knowing we work with you.

The work of the previous level was to clear any karmic bondage you carried from past conditioning and to free yourself to explore your creative consciousness. You have come through that activity and are moving with the intensity of that creative consciousness.

Be in humbleness with your own being, for your instruments and thoughts and mind flows with the higher power and actualizes your true being, realized through divine love.

Walk with the understanding of Solomon and with the silence and wisdom of the Christ. The journey is an on going movement of an eternal unfoldment. Be in love and in watchfulness of your consciousness. Go in peace.

Lesson Twenty Six

COLOR RAY: VIOLET-PURPLE LIGHT

Will

Message

Yes, this is Jove. I speak with the wisdom of your being and the wisdom of the hierarchy and that which is to present you with the desired action of which the light is an implant of your own conscious self. You are being prepared to empower your nature with a positive effect in this term of your journey through life. The empowering effect is the connection of your center and base of the life force to the totality of your inner and outer being.

Within this lesson, you work in the radiant Violet-Purple Ray in which *the will* is the center and core of your physical awakening. The desire of the causal self is connected to this center. The Kundalini Fire is empowered with the magnified consciousness of the Scarlet Ray.

Let us speak further on what you perceive as the initiatory experience. Many within this path of light are approaching the end of the cycles of lives within the earth journey. They are accelerating individual growth into acceptance of self in pure service to the earth as manifestors of the light in the activity of full healing power. Know that the empowering of the healing consciousness is a most important part of your service to that which comes in effect, for you are on the brink of experiences that cannot be fully prepared for in the conscious way.

The changes in humanity will begin to erupt in unusual form. Mental depression becomes a part of the purifying aspect, as mental depression becomes an act of rebellion against the spirit. But as you work with those under depressed and repressed energy, you begin to unlock the key that hides the fear that overrides their activity of joy. You begin to act as intermediates and intercessors for those who cannot see the way except as blindness and death.

You open the way to the door to realities where there is a life expectancy of a total new realm of experience and yes, physically, as well as spiritually. The physical plane is still a part of the divine plan that moves into its accelerated and elevated state.

There will be those of you who leave without the death as known to a normal physical experience. There will be others working in survival activities, helping process what has been a purged experience. There will be others who are absolute enlightened ones who create the way for the law to be presented in spirit and soul in a human expression. You have many things to move through before you have completed your individual journeys, and your process will bring you into a higher expression of soul integration.

All the work of light is a key factor presenting humanity with alternatives in which the international systems become a new communicative experience. There are healings transpiring at multi-levels, as well as the counter-force that would oppose the system for its freeing activity. The Christ energy is in the earth. It has been with man through all ages, but is now predominant in many different faces.

There are those who have attained a cosmic enlightened state and there are those who guide others into a pathway to self-realization. There are also those who are hidden in the cloak of deceit, who would appear to be the apostles and the Christ. They come as oppressors to deviate the path of truth and the discernment will come as a difficult lesson.

Do not be quick to follow what appears as power under material orders. Begin to recognize that The Christ is hidden from any material form. The Christ exists in the simplistic vibration of truth. The Christ exists as the Oversoul in which the energy of love is exuberant and flowing.

You will know the way when you experience the energy of love interrelating with the memory of the divine love of self. You will not be deceived if you follow that which is true in regard to practicality and in regard to assimilation of wisdom and knowledge.

Many things occur as there are tumultuous changes arising. I, Jove, speak of this in order for you to know that you do not walk in vain with these experiences of light, that it is not a conflict with what you hold as the positive force to bring healing into consciousness. You are all healers and your healing will be empowered by the rays of light.

As you touch the heart of another, you awaken the lotus blossom within the chakra of that vibration. When you meet the deceiver, turn away from that experience, and yet leave the thread of love in the concerned and the discerned ego, you have implanted a seed that can open that form to self-realization.

Do not feel you fail when those who have seen you, walk away in discouragement. Do not feel you have been in a negative expression if you are not seen, heard or touched by what you desire to give. Those who rebel and resist must have their own moment of awakening.

We perceive through movement of consciousness, there is a tremendous wave of new energy active through many different forms of experience. We perceive in the musical realm, tremendous incorporation of sounds that bring about a new listening ear that is appeasing to the mind and pleasing to the soul, a refreshment to the physical and a joy to the heart. We perceive new sounds integrating high spherical energy into unusual movements that begin a process of opening consciousness in the mental plane.

We perceive that there are many different waves of activity of new thought that merge in different experiences of life. We perceive in the physical and medical fields, avenues of openness to new alternatives in healing.

All has been spoken before and yet is in the wave of its own arrival. I, Jove have been an overseer of the movement of this particular divine plan incorporated for the openness of the human mind.

Each one of you is a teacher and a servant. You are an instigator for greater good. Each of you, in your own individual way, begins to awaken the pathway for another soul to find the keys to its inner peace.

In this work of light, there is no sense of being in a negative frame. It is all a joyous pathway to another level of your own experience. While the road may seem difficult, while obstacles may appear and the testing of self is done through many different experiences, it is all a process bringing you into a greater expression.

Meditation Process

Once again, come to experience the power from the Council of Light as it is directed to bring about the connection of one center to another, connecting the Kundalini to the higher planes and through all the soul vibration. Magnify the energies and experience the feeling of love and fulfillment, balance and completeness moving in and throughout the emotional system.

Let go of all false thoughts, impressions and instincts, and the negative vibrations projected to you from outside sources, releasing any negativity from psychic consciousness. Once again, you are enveloped in this beautiful sphere and magnetic field of the vibrant White Light as you move through the centers activating each chakra.

Perceive the vibration of the Golden Ray directed throughout the unconscious and the conscious self, raising the energy and vibratory rate of the body and all of its many parts. Simply experience yourself being lifted in this radiant energy. Let go of all thoughts of mental confusion and mental warring.

Move into the center of the Wisdom Ray and perceive the frequency of this light directed into the cells and consciousness of the cellular structure in the body. If there remain any fears, traumas, judgments, release them. Reaffirm that wisdom and knowing comes into a conscious acceptance.

Moving through the center of the Emerald Green activate this ray. Merge into the center of the Violet-Purple Ray. This frequency is expressed throughout the total being as an activator to bring conditions into motion for accepting your destiny, your path, your purpose, your goals and deepest desires.

Reaffirm that it is all now in fullness. Activate all of the soul centers as we move from the physical dimension, the third dimensional plane.

Rise up through the Rainbow Bridge of light and take a moment to bathe in the Silver Light. Reaffirm you are nurtured, you are fulfilled and you are complete as your subjective self is balanced with your dynamic.

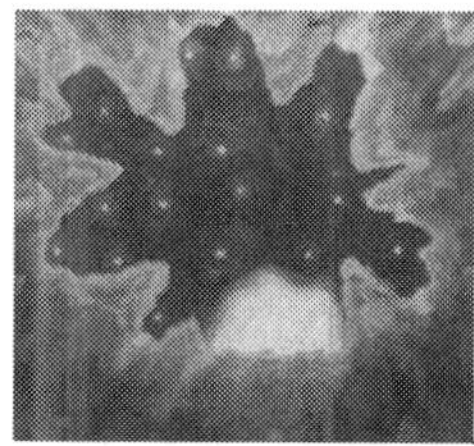Artist Kathy Nadalin

Rise up and move into the planetary center in consciousness once again, joining with the Council of Light to greet the teachers and the masters. Whatever vibration is ready to communicate with your experience and expression, prepare in the silence to meet the ascended teachers and experience their vibration and their presence.

You will find intense energy moving from the base of the spine up through the total physical plane, to the heart chakra, to the will center and to the mind-thought.

Connection occurs through the intervention of the mind of the higher self and your conscious expression, in which personality egoism itself is a participant.

Again, the actuality and the technicalities cannot be fully observed, for they become more than the self can truly incorporate in its minute vibration. But, the visual effect is you become enveloped in this light, in the rays of the Violet-Purple Ray and soul energy is infused with the consciousness of this vibrant, vital force. As soul is infused in the frequency of this light, it is directed to connect with the core at the base of your own physical being, at the lower spine, the chakra of the flame of which the Scarlet Ray is activated.

You will experience tremendous awakening beyond what you have thought in the past. It will refresh the mind, it will open the dream state and it will integrate within a sensibility of you. Fear not change; accept it as a viable part of your full consciousness. Each of you in your own individual way will find that key of peace. . . .

Silence

When you have completed the integration with the Kundalini Fire energy for this session, prepare for your own grounding.

**Go now and may the light of the Christ be in
and through you.**

Lesson Twenty Seven

COLOR RAY: RUBY RED

Healing

"The more you work through the angers and
denials within the lower plane, the more you begin
to vibrate on the higher frequencies in the inner
levels."

Message

We speak to you in this session regarding the interpersonal relationship, interpersonal communication, the vibrations of love energy and the biological systems that are in correspondence to an inner expression.

As you incarnated, you received this life as an opportunity to bring balance into past conditions and to integrate the lessons of humanity in earth. You have experienced the lessons of human negation as well as human elation. Your soul chose to function in this plane to glorify a consciousness of love.

Through the many different pathways, there has been activity of being blinded by egos such as envy, jealousy, sorrow, sadness and dis-ease. All of these imageries exist by the creation of human consciousness.

You have choices to make, either give power to these perceived imageries and accept them as your own lessons or rise above these conditions to states of consciousness where you give yourself to the vibrations of higher thought and divine essence. The love you seek to express is far beyond human behavior, yet manifested through human activity.

You have many choices in your desire to express the *Love Principle*. Each one who enters your life path can become an important student, teacher or correspondent in the lessons of love. The heartaches, the heartbreaks, the sorrows and pains have manifested through self-centeredness of lower egos. Release yourself from these harbored pains, and bring yourself into the light.

Meditation Process

Focus your awareness completely into the center of the heart chakra, your emotional plane and begin to perceive yourself as freeing your consciousness from intimidation, fear aspects, separateness, indecisiveness, loss and rejection.

Once again, know rejection is an image that appears real to the personal self, but in actuality, it is a consciousness of being separate from your own spirit. Another cannot reject you, but you reject your own being.

Each of you has the power to uplift another, to raise the vibrations and to use these energies as tools to clear the physical body of denied imagery. Act out of that consciousness from that point of love within the heart of your own being.

Think and be, for nothing is impossible. Know that all things are connections and networked through spirit and through Mind.

Nothing can deter you from your own higher expression, except for the belief in the obstacles and denial factors as reality.

When completeness is felt by integrating, by being in wholeness, there is only the wisdom of communications with those who are in correspondence to the lessons presented to your own consciousness. No one walks away without a reason. You are not left by another's rejection. You are simply passing through certain systems of consciousness and moving towards different pathways of understanding and growth.

Perceive now the vibrancy of the Ruby Red Light as it clears all activity within the emotional plane. Perceive your emotional body restoring its inner wounds by manifesting a true understanding of the consciousness of love. Love is without judgment, love is without any pain, and love is without any fear. Love knows no sorrow. Love expresses, integrates, uplifts and heals.

Those who are the subjects of animosity, from within your own being, transmute the image. Look at those who have been a source of anger and negation and uplift them, lifting self within the essence of the Ruby Ray. Perceive the anger and hostilities released from within your own spirit and the physical consciousness.

The more you work through these angers and denials within the lower plane, the more you begin to vibrate on the higher frequencies in the inner levels. The effectiveness of your power will be felt through the healing that you send forth.

Now each of you let the light, the frequency of the Ruby Red Ray, become an energy flow through every system of your own physical senses. Perceive that the body egos and all systems within the physical self are enveloped in the energy ray of this vibrant, healing activity. Let love be the source of your upliftment and healing. Perceive this frequency also being directed to those who have caused pain and revenge and discordant activity.

Judge not, simply release their hold on your consciousness and let yourself be freed from their imageries. All of you have seen and felt the angers and the bitterness of conflict and war. All have felt the heart torn into its shattered consciousness. But now let go and bless each one and let light and the consciousness of love be the source of all healing.

Perceive now, those who have reflected the beauty of your own consciousness and call forth those who are in correspondence to the flame of love within your own conscious self. See them receiving the light. Perceive them as an open communication.

All too often, the human ego has been crushed by judgments and by those who stand as overbearing power systems. Let the consciousness accept itself as an expression of light and love, seeing the joy and beauty of its true nature and feeding the conscious self with the positive energy to bring about the greatness which you can become as you unfold in your individual evolution.

Know that whatever may appear as a flaw within your expression is but an image to be molded into a new expression. These flaws are the challenges for greater growth. Forgive yourself. Feel the heart and the warmth and love of your nature. It is much easier to deny self, to spew forth the imperfections, to look at the negations, the lacks, and the limiting factors and to accept behavior systems that create the guilt, but it is much greater to see self in a light of love and perfection.

In your personal meditations, allow yourself to experience the reaching out to touch the hearts of those who are caught in their pain. Simply see the heart as perfect and the emotional body released from its lower, denser consciousness. Fear denies the soul's expression—love communicates that sense of oneness.

Again, as you serve and as you release, so also are you lifted. The Christ walks amongst you, both as spirit and as man. Awaken self to the coming of His vibration. Feel His call to your heart, letting go all sense of unworthiness.

Perceive your energy merging with all within this circle of light as we call forth the souls and egos of all who are working towards the manifestation of higher consciousness. We call forth all students to send the work of light to all beings that are choosing to walk a path of growth, a path of service and a path of love.

Be all focused as one expression, one vibration enveloping each student of light. Perceive each student enveloped in love and the healing energy of the Ruby Red Ray. Call forth all of those who would rise up the consciousness of the planet.

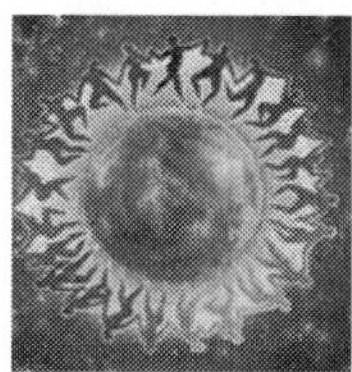

Perceive yourself in a network of light directing this frequency through all systems of consciousness. See the earth enveloped in light. The heart of the earth, which is the heart of man, is broken, despondent. Heal the heart.

When you are ready, call forth your egos back into the forebrain; call your consciousness back into the physical body. Out of the love of your being will come the healing power. Without love, there is nothing; without mind, there could be no creation.

Unify your mind, your conscious self and all that you are with the love of your being. Be physicians, be the source of healing consciousness and be at peace. Be prepared to experience love completely. The symbol of the rose is the symbol of the heart in its perfection, in its perfect bloom. Its many petals of perfect design are a fragrance and essence of love.

Go in peace and let The Christ dwell within your own heart.

From the channel ...

The cd will bring you through the integration with the Kundalini Fire energy.

Lesson Twenty Eight

COLOR RAY: ORANGE

Perceptual

"With clear perception, awakening of clear sight,
there is a re-alignment of all situations."

Message

Greetings, this is Azreal.

The earth's perceptual body is very murky and extremely distorted. There is little within the perceptual body of the earth planet that is of a positive state.

With clear perception, awakening of clear sight, there is a re-alignment of all situations. The veils of darkness that hover within the perceptual being are very dense. Let your mind move with the idea of cleansing the perceptual being of the earth's body. Its perceptual aura is a direct result of the perceptions of the living entities within itself.

If the collective thought of the human race sees the earth destroying itself by becoming more violent, more warlike, more hungry, more confused, more detached and more separated, then the perception of the collective mind is in the down path of evolution.

Perceive the natural resources in balance with the needs of all individuals. Hunger and thirst, poverty and sickness and elements of human degradation are results of separateness in consciousness and misperceived activity.

Visualize the perception and the visual expression of the collective energy of the humanity seeing heaven actualized in the earth. Visualize energy patterns of food, shelter and human needs fulfilled to those in hunger and loss of shelter.

Affirm that perfect balance is now manifesting in all areas of the earth's living body. Perceive the elimination of wastes and pollution. Perceive the corrections of cancerous activities within the earth's body, man's interference in the total scheme of the earth's evolution.

Now perceive the natural resources are in balance with the needs of all individuals. Hunger and thirst, poverty and sickness and all elements of human degradation are results of separateness in consciousness and misperceived activity. Think of the mind of human beings and the perceptual natures of all minds coming into clear vision, into clear consciousness, into cosmic sense, into the spirit of love, and focusing on the highest potential for human experience.

Meditation Process

In this session, activate the frequency of the Radiant Orange Light, the frequency of your psychic nature, the intuitive, perceptual, instinctive consciousness. Feel its vibration moving in and through the body, concentrating within the nervous system.

Merge and greet the Council of Light, the Great White Brotherhood and those who are a part of the work to bring about changes in the evolving of the collective human race and your individual journey into soul fusion. Let your guidance direct you through the networking of light. The ray of the Radiant Orange frequency magnifies and connects with the process of healing.

Be still and know, all things are in their proper order according to your own being. Trust the inner knowing that guides you through changes within yourself. Trust in your sense of direction.   As you incorporate the laws and principles of spiritual enlightenment, you walk in an essence of compatibility with your own inner being.

Gather your egos and with awareness rise up through the Rainbow Bridge into the center of your higher being, the planetary vibration. Recognize you are, by thought, transcending the planes of the physical, moving into a vibration rate that is faster and of higher frequencies leading you into an essence, which is part of Cosmic Sense.

As you perceive yourself moving through the rays of light into the inner temple, in consciousness accept with openness, freedom the presence of counselors. It is true that a counselor of light does perceive much of your individual experiences, never interfering, but rejoicing in the awakening.

With each of your egos gathered into this center of consciousness, perceive your vibrations as forms of energy emitting the radiant frequency of the Orange Ray. Much information regarding the purpose and essence of this vibration is received regarding its connection to the nervous system and raising the perceptual consciousness into expanded sensitivity.

Azreal

Yes, I greet you with the light, the wisdom and the spirit. In this experience, you are receiving cosmic rays of light. If you have any distortions of yourself infuse these with the energy of the Orange Ray of light

We perceive your physical body transforming moving structurally, emotionally, mentally, and within the astral body, blending more with soul and higher self. Each step presents lessons to you, relating to the effects of the ideas of who you are, and relating to the joy that your heart desires to experience.

We speak on soul infusion. The inner work activated through the multi-dimensional is a process in which the clearing within the soul-causal nature is first brought into accelerated activity. Clearing within the soul-causal body is a necessity before there can be a full infusion of the Kundalini Fire energy to the lower self.

All in this path of light moves through phases in this planetary system where the soul-causal body experiences the intensity of energy releasing karmic causes of its past action. You no longer are connected into the reincarnation system from this point in this path of light. You are on a level in which the law and principles of divine love are now an active part of your mental, emotional and perceptual consciousness.

You can return to the wheel of karma by entanglements that hold you in repetitive patterns, but the psychic chains have been broken and the released from the past. Therefore, soul infusion with the Kundalini Fire Energy is the step in the process toward Angelic Awareness.

With the ray of Scarlet Light, with the activation of the Kundalini Fire energy, with the flow of this life force moving throughout your system and cosmic rays activated into your total beingness, you are receiving intense acceleration on all planes. It is not a matter of believing it is a matter of knowing. It is simply an act in which the process occurs.

The full pattern is ot be revealed, as that unfolds in its own time within your own awareness. It is all in the making and the unfolding. The time of its full acceptance is within the framework of your individual patterns. What has begun within this level is a continuous process until completion has occurred. Completion may take a period from weeks to months to years to lifetime experience. The degree of receiving divine love is the culmination and beginning of entering into Cosmic Consciousness and into the acceleration of self into yet a higher domain of expression.

The soul infusion completes when you no longer find yourself in states of warring, anxiety, fear, restlessness and disease. When "the peace that passes all understanding," is realized on all planes, you may experience Cosmic Consciousness. There are only a few Christed, enlightened masters, who experience the infusion of the soul to Cosmic Sense. There are few within the collective humanity who had any part to play in that expression, but through the beings of light, the workers of light and the interconnection between the hierarchy and yourself, the probable course of Cosmic Consciousness may be attained.

You cannot read your way into the dimension of this experience; you cannot intellectualize yourself into becoming a cosmically aware entity. It is a matter of the destined point of your inner and outer self. Through the council we create a communication system transmitting the energy to those who are ready to receive and express.

Once again, the vibration and rays of the Kundalini fire energy rises up through the bodies magnified and activated within the chakra of the Radiant Orange Ray. Experience its power as it draws all negativity to itself to consume it in the light and rises like fire from within to without.   Breathe deeply as you go into a silence.

 **Silver** Left, **Gold** Right, **Ruby Red** Back,

Orange Front, **White** base

When your awareness returns you are drawn back to your own physical plane, perceive a radiant pyramid of light, a beautiful structure symmetrically aligned to all the planes based on the triangles and all its many additions.   This healing pyramid becomes, once again, the chamber of your own individual mind. The pyramids are a force field of energy in which you function individually, healing your own consciousness, as well as those who are a part of your everyday experiences.

In this session, utilize the healing pyramid with the Radiant Silver on the magnetic and the Radiant Gold on the dynamic.   Perceive the essence of the Ruby Red in the back and the Radiant Orange across the front.   Fill in the base with the White Light. Bring all of your friends, family and loved ones into the pyramid of light for their healing.

As you complete your own meditation within this sacred place, seal the force field by activating the light in a clockwise motion.

Feel the bodies responding with greater flexibility and lightness and healing as you close your meditation

Go in peace and may the light of the Christ be in and through you.

Lesson Twenty Nine

COLOR RAY: PINK

Divine Love

Message

It is most important for each of you to understand the intensities that are activated in and throughout the planet earth are for the purpose of restoring perfection of the spirit in the human soul and human element.

It is important that you as the beings of light, are the visual energy to create the effect in which this can unfold. You are each being imbued with much love in order to create the acceptance within your being to the opportunity to serve in this most gracious way.

The empowering of your vibration has been an active action throughout this course of expression. You have each been individually under the consciousness of the vibration of the masters. You have each journeyed through the fears and journeyed through resistance into joy in accordance to the level of the moment of your mind. You are still in the process of coming into that internal state where the strength of self is fully actualized by the rays of light.

You have found the essences of your being in much conflict with the outer form. You have found your beingness in detriment in accordance to the vibrations of those you meet in your daily experience, but look not to the pain and experience the power of the divinity of light. Perceive the light integrated throughout each of the consciousness of you as a source of love.

Meditation Process

Follow your meditation process moving into the Planetary Center.

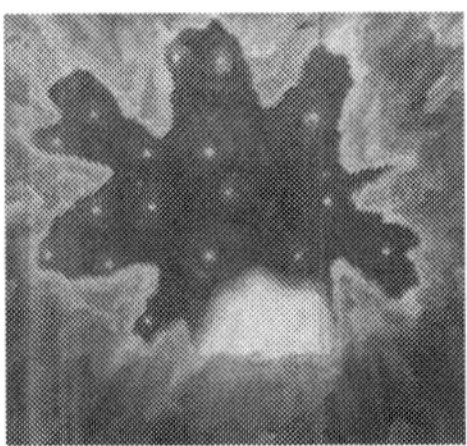

Greetings, this is Azreal

As I speak, perceive that the body, form, humanness, egoism and identities are enveloped in the rays where energy internalizes within the system of your expression. Perceive from the base of the spine, the energy of power, the life force, being magnified and directed throughout your physical body.

Empowering means to strengthen. Empowering means to create opportunity to express. Empowering means to open the door to the level in which soul, mind and spirit become infused as one. Whatever barriers exist, perceive them released. Infusing the power with divine love is the ultimate union within body and self-being.

You now begin to feel the flame of light moving throughout the body's consciousness up and through the physical head area, spiraling in and about your total system, bringing the negative from the spine up and through the head vibration, empowering the body with the love divine. To focus from this experience is to accept the record of your own soul as released from inversion, denial and pain.

It is most difficult for each of you to know love, to accept love, to know yourself as love. While the words are spoken over and over, the reality becomes distorted by the patterns of the past that hold your energy in the level of unworthiness, in the remembrances of self-resistance, in the neglect of your consciousness to know spirit and soul as one. Re-instate, re-accept, re-affirm and re-implant.

You are brought to this point for definite reasons—changes involving group experiences are now in effect. Individually, you become a center of light. Individually, you become overseers of many students who look to your consciousness as a source of healing. Individually, you begin the path to your highest aspirations as you draw into your consciousness those who are in need of light and healing. Collectively, you become as one unit under the Order of Melchizedek, under the council that decrees each of you into your personal life experience.

Fear not what appears as the tumultuous changes, they are more internal than external. The external changes are environmental energy flow, cosmic rays directed to the earth for the purpose of its cleansing, transmutation and integration. Cataclysmic energy is breaking up stagnation, security systems are changing, leaderships moving out and the new coming in. Prophecies of the past come into focus. Be stable and strong for the change will bring a joyous event into the physical experience.

Reach out and touch all through the network of light sending the message of peace. Direct your light.

Each of you once again perceives your consciousness one with the network of energy. Many have desired to release themselves from the earth to find themselves in other planes, desiring to let go of their presence within this system, but your day of transition does not come until you are ready on all planes. You have asked and committed to love and to walk in light.

From this moment through time you are souls ancient gathered from past experience to present and to future time. You work collectively as a part of light expression.

When you return to your centers, you once again perceive the structure of the pyramid in and around you. As you activate a sacred space, bring all into this energy field where you gather with all friends, family and those in need.

As student-initiates, you have accepted your work, your lessons and your commitment. When you are complete with this process in light, ground your energy and experience the flow of light moving down through you body, through your feet and into the Black Power Center.

Go in peace and may the light and the wisdom of the Christ be in and through you.

Lesson Thirty

COLOR RAY: AMETHYST

Peaceful Warrior

"Without conflict, the stagnation of self occurs.
Without a sense of conflict, there could be no
understanding of peace."

Message

It has been a while since I have communicated with you in a verbal sense, but I, Jove, speak that you may know the presence is still amongst the brethren of light and that each of you may know once again this vibrant ego which speaks to all who would have the openness to receive.

Perceive the earth enveloped in this essence to dissipate the many factions that would separate man from his own evolving being. Remember, dear students, that the stresses and warring nature brings forth a new awakening. Without conflict, the stagnation of occurs.

The pressures of change appear as factions of war. In essence, they are preparing for yet new understanding and new expansions. In all areas of mind, there must be the warring nature that brings forth the new life. Without a sense of conflict, there could be no understanding of peace.

As your mind dwells on the warring forces within the planet and centers on certain areas, think of all of the minds as a collective consciousness. Think of all entities as one mass of collective thought and surround it with the essence of this vibrant ray. Whether it be the revolutions in foreign countries or within the area of your own being, the light is activated, magnified and released.

Travels in time to altered states can be fascinating to the personality self. Know that as your personality experiences a connection to these inner levels of thought, it is rejoicing in its own understanding. Do not deny the personality. Allow it to be uplifted.

There is much work to do, not only through world and universal service, but also within the individual systems. Again, beloved students, the masters of light understand the difficulties in applying what is experienced on the inner planes to outer daily life. At times, you may question your effectiveness in service to others when there is yet unfinished business within the life lived in the body, but do not lose your sense of direction or faith.

What you give forth from your consciousness becomes a reward in every aspect. As spoken in the past, I, Jove, reach out to touch those who teach others not only of the light, but also of systems of thought that can bring forth new awakenings.

Meditation

Quickly focus your awareness into the center of your own soul vibration. As you are aware through the practice, the gathering up of your vibration is a very individual experience. At this point in your continuing progression and evolution, thought brings forth consciousness quickly, instantaneously, as the egos become acclimated to moving in a unified manner.

As your thought moves through the centers of light, feel the essence of each vibration, each frequency activated along the central vertical axis.

With your awareness, move up through the Silver Ray and the Rainbow Bridge to the planetary center of light.

Each of you move once more into the temples of learning, into the temples of wisdom, perceiving your individual spirit enveloped in the raiment of light, moving in unison with your own master teachers of which there are many. The unification takes place between your consciousness and the inner guides of your own being.

Let go of all consciousness within the physical plane. Some of you are still holding on to the physical. Let go and move into the centers within the planetary consciousness. Move in unity of mind, body and spirit.

At this moment in time, we bring you into a center in which you can receive direction regarding the work within this frequency ray. Previously, you have been told this energy ray dissipates the dis-eases within the body. It is the warring vibration that sets up a protection against conflicting forces. It is an activator of imageries within your own conscious being. This frequency is to be used when you are seeking to dissipate any conflict that may be occurring within your own individual consciousness, or those warring conflicts that deter your evolution.

Your body, your physical self, reacts to this vibration in many unique ways. Often, reactions may occur that would bring forth dis-ease from past conditions, as the purifying aspect moves through the body.

Each of you, focus your awareness and consciousness as one mind and one being preparing to direct the consciousness of light into the planet earth.

Do not look upon this vibrant Amethyst energy as a negative experience, but as an up lifter. See as an energy that brings one out of stages of passivity into an awareness of greater expansion.

Let the masters, merge with your Mind. Receive the love and connection. Free yourself from all limiting concepts, for here in this level there is no dissension or separation.

Now perceive yourselves expanded in the Amethyst vibration. Move through the networks of light to direct this frequency into the aura within the earth level. Perceive the earth receiving your frequency for expansion and evolution, that which brings forth the age of truth. Know you are part of many who are working through the stages of self-transformation to create an expanded world of light and love.

Think of your Mind as vehicles in which movement occurs simply by thought. Wherever you desire to be, there you arrive. Where you desire to serve, there you become a part of that service, just as the masters of light, in the twinkling of an eye can move through space. Think on these things.

As your Mind dwells on the warring forces within the planet and centers on certain areas, think of all of the Minds as a collective consciousness. Think of all entities as one mass of collective thought and surround it with the essence of this vibrant Amethyst

Ray. Whether it is the revolutions in foreign countries or within your own being, the light is activated, magnified and released.

Travels in time to altered states can be fascinating to the personality self. Know that as your personality experiences a connection to these inner levels of thought, it is rejoicing in its own understanding. Do not deny the personality. Allow it to be uplifted.

There is much work to be done, not only through world and universal service, but also within the individual systems. Again, beloved students, the masters of light understand the difficulties in applying what is experienced on the inner planes to outer daily life. At times, you may question your effectiveness in service to others when there is yet unfinished business within the life lived in the body, but do not lose your sense of direction or faith.

What you give forth from your consciousness becomes a reward in every aspect. As spoken in the past, I, Jove, reach out to touch those who teach others not only of the light, but also of systems of thought that can bring forth new awakenings.

You are one of many moving through the changes of time, the changes of consciousness and the changes of direction. It is most important to allow the individual spirit to be expressed, to allow the love to come forth uninhibited and to experience unity and motives of all as one Christed body, the embodiment of the life force of The Christed self. The movement towards wholeness, while individual, is yet as many. Think on these things.

Gold on left, Silver on right, Pink in Back, Amethyst in front, white at the base.

When your consciousness is totally within your centers and you are feeling a sense of joy from the inner work and the clearings that are taking place, activate the radiant pyramid around your consciousness and field of activity. Draw into this pyramid those individuals who are in most need of healing, love, peace and truth.

Feel the vibrations of the pyramidal structure, vibrantly activated in the Radiant Gold and Silver on the left and right sides, the Radiant Pink Ray in back with the Amethyst in front. Bring the White Light up from the base to finish creating this force field.

Experience its balance as the love flows with the vibrancy of the warrior light. Feel their unity. Magnify the light and affirm perfection in and through all levels of yourself if the body becomes heavy or in dis-ease.

It is a truth, "heaven is a state of being that exists as a place of total harmony." One arrives at that moment when spirit, mind and body are in complete and perfect unity when spirit, mind and body function as one experience, as one flowing harmony, when the tones are all blending in their highest frequencies.

To dwell in this state of Mind, while simultaneously walking in the physical plane, seems to be impossible. Yet, each one can experience those qualities within your life path. To be centered and encompassed in the perfection of the highest level of consciousness.

You will flow with peace and harmony within your physical activity while others seem to operate in mental confusion, fear and disarray. You will stand as a magnet of loving thoughts and harmonious minds attuned to the realities of the spiritual concepts. Your work will be a total expression of the highest ideals.

When you have completed your meditation ground your thoughts, feelings and energy through the body and down through the legs and out the feet. Anchor your experience through the Black Power Center.

Go in peace and may the light unify all parts of your being.

From the channel ...

The cd will take you through the integration of the Kundalini Fire Energy.

Lesson Thirty One

COLOR RAY: MINT GREEN

Rejuvenation

"In order to transform the total systems, begin
within self and then move into the group
experience, transforming group experience into
new births, new life and new expressions."

Message

I, Azreal, speak to each of you in your dream states, often coming in moments of stress or moments of enlightenment.

I am often expressing in a form of light through a thought, a vibration in an element of peace, in a time for comfort and in a time for discipline.

Often, the embodiment of the vibration is in and throughout your individual consciousness as well as others who are part of the council.

Think in terms of the masters, not so much as personified individuals but as Beings in Mind functioning to connect you with a new understanding with elevated states of consciousness.

Who are the guides and who are the masters?

There are many never recognized, for they remain unidentified. Nonetheless, they exist as beings within the plane of soul activity. Many of you have recognized a Presence surrounding you. Often you begin to feel communication or an experience of sensory knowing there is a Spirit activity transpiring.

How do you know what your higher self desires to express? How do you know when free will interfere in the nature of the greater self? How can you discern between purpose and destiny for growth and integration, and what is manifesting through self-consciousness and personality?

Discernment comes through internalizing inner peace through whatever you are acting upon. When there is an inner peace, there is a strength beyond intellect and reason. When there is a focal point stemming from your insight and instinct, you are following the process and purpose of your higher self.

Each life presents many activities and effects of past consciousness. Many patterns of past conditioning must be broken in order to receive a transformed consciousness. When old patterns manifest consistently and re-cycle through your every-day experience, you have resisted a transformation of your inner consciousness. In order to bring the new there must be the letting-go of resistance of old actions.

Each of you asked within yourself about the nature of their being, their reality, their existence and their influence. We spoke often of the many within the Brotherhood of Light under the Order of Melchizedek. As you have groups in the path of light through *A Course in Light* there are groups of teachers and masters connected to your energy flow who experience through you, activity of unfoldment within their own expression.

At these moments, do not fear and do not become confused. Understand, guidance is given as an inner connection to your own soul.

Meditation Process

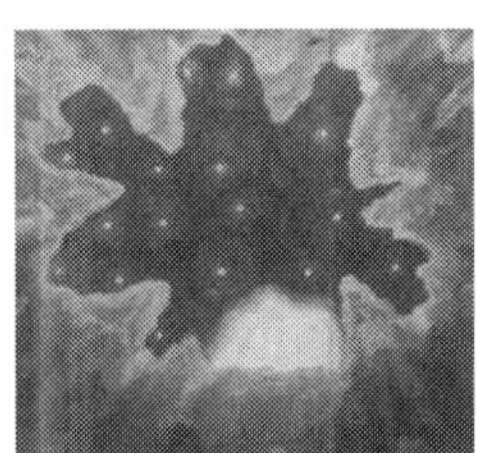 Artist Kathy Nadalin

This is Azreal speaking again to each of you personally and in a very distinct manner. Rise up with your thought into the center of light within the soul plane and meet your guides and teachers so you may emanate sensitivity to their presence and experience their merging with your vibration.

In this session, as you are embodied in the vibrations of the Radiant Mint Green Light, perceive this frequency actuating new energy throughout the total systems. In your individual self, begin to feel your bodies revitalizing within the cellular element and the organic element. Perceive your physical totally immersed within this vibration.

Now rise up through the soul plane to the hierarchy, into the planetary center. Trust and know that all is of right thought. Growth comes through every moment of your existence. Growth, expansion, new life, new joy and new activity are results of awakened awareness.

Resistance occurs through the fear within the personality. Resistance to growth is fear of the unknown. When growth is stagnating, there becomes a cesspool of negativity. In order to clear the stagnation, open your total senses to new life, new understandings, new direction and new expansion.

Life is a journey you desire to experience. Do not fear it!

Now, perceive the essence of this Radiant Mint Green Ray is manifesting in and through the total earth   Perceive the earth born with a new attitude of consciousness, new vitality, rejuvenation and new inspiration.

Perceive the earth not as a stagnant ball of energy disintegrating, destroying and dying through the embers of anger, conflict or self-negation. Perceive the life force is once again bathing the earth in new elements of consciousness, bathing the total system in a new nature of activity. See it spring forth into a vibrant experience of cleansing, clarity and beauty.

Pollution of mind, pollution of spirit, pollution of materiality, all cloaks the new growth. Those who can visualize and accept a new generation and a new rejuvenation can see the earth radiating in new forms of experience. Perceive the earth reborn into a new vibration and this frequency manifesting throughout all the earth.

The aura of the earth is very much like the aura of your individual self. The earth's vibrations emanate very much as your individual consciousness.

In order for transformation to be complete, begin within self and then move into the group consciousness, transforming group experience into new births, new life and new expressions.

In order for the Age of Aquarius consciousness to come into its full bloom, individuals must be ready to see with new eyes and hear with new ears. They must accept the vibrations of a higher consciousness.

The light work transpired through this system of energy consciousness for unifying you with your transformed self. All of the lightwork takes you through the cycles of your past into the present. The constant repetition of old patterns must be recognized to clear away the reactions and to create the new vibration.

When Jesus the Christ raised up out of the physical earth body, He activated this particular energy of the Mint Green frequency to transmute the total physical body into a higher and finer energy consciousness. The masters who taught the secrets of the light force gave the tools of which He used. Much can be revealed through ancient records that were lost because of the minds of those who could not accept this reality and desecrated the wisdom inherent within these records.

Now move with awareness through the network of light. Become united with the many sources of light, wisdom, joy and upliftment. Feel the force moving through the entire network. Perceive a new earth, a new activity.

Move with awareness into areas within the planet cloaked in the prejudice. Think of nations that cling to systems that deny the freedoms of individual experience and perceive yourself as the Mind directing light to free these patterns.

Direct light into the earth's crest and into those troubled areas, which are under pressure and about to erupt. Perceive this essence of light moving into those systems to release the vibrations of pressure. Perceive the earth not destroyed, but renewed.

When you feel your conscious self-desiring to experience newness of the egos, move back into the physical plane through the centers of the Radiant Silver ray into the White light of the soul center. Perceive the soul enveloped in the essence of the Radiant Mint Green energy. Perceive the mental plane in balance with the consciousness of new life, joy and unity. These processes and projections for greater good are for many individuals.

You are the birth of an idea, a concept of an experience moving in this time and place, for change and evolution.

Be the light. Experience this energy as your beacon, your tool and as your sword.

Now move into the soul center of your own consciousness and feel yourself coming into a new awakening, into new joy, into new excitement, expression, growth and activity. Expand yourself.

As you stand focused, completely centered within your own being, experience inner strength, tranquility and sensitivity, knowing you are a light movement against all obstacles that deny the greater good.

282

Silence

As you complete your inner process bring the light in and through all of the your body. Activate the power center of the Black Ray.[8]

From the channel ...

The cd activates the Kundalini Fire Energy process.

---

[8] cd

Lesson Thirty Two

COLOR RAY: SCARLET

Passion

"The movement of the Christ Spirit is magnified
within the earth uplifting those ready to see its
impact on individual life."

Message

The disciplines given to challenge your consciousness have been intense. There are yet still challenges ahead and the trust factor must be instilled and undefined.

All of the preceding lessons brought you through many different levels of consciousness to a place of clearing the entanglements of all karmic imbalances. The process of dislodging your energy from former activities has been very intense. Now, in your personal meditations affirm that you are releasing indebtedness to all concerned, both in present and past consciousness.

The initiatory process is a very difficult journey through change. This intensified activity brings the selves of all of the lower bodies into a mirror of its own expression. Each individual will come into recognition of its true self through the internalization of the light and through the activity of the desire from the higher self.

Know that each stage of development is an important realization to both the inner self and to the conscious self. Each phase and cycle of the path of light contains energies, which break through the resistances of all past negations.

Some may ask, what is the Christ Spirit? What is the Christ incarnate? What is the Christ personified? What is the Christ consciousness? The Christ Spirit is the light of the highest order of hierarchy within Higher Mind. The Christ Spirit is Divine Love.

Christ Consciousness is awareness of moving, breathing, and living as an expression of Divine Love. Christ Consciousness is living within the Law of spiritual principles. Christ Consciousness is a part of Cosmic Consciousness. Christ incarnate is the Consciousness of the Creator Father incarnated as the son, Jesus the Christ. The movement of the Christ Spirit is magnified within the earth and uplifting those ready for impact on individual lives.

To love as Christ loves is beyond all human expression. It is love that sees from the inner self to the outer plane. It is love that knows no separateness and only the acceptance of the divine consciousness individualized through every entity.

The acceleration is moving quickly through the human egoism. The conflict between the evolutionary and involution is magnified in an intensified activity.

Therefore, know that you will stand firm on what you know as the highest good, both within self and as a collective whole. The call comes to stand forth and claim the birthright of your consciousness as a son of light and to claim your identity with the universal forces that bring forth the greater expression into all systems.

Meditation Process

Greetings, this is Azreal. We speak to you with the light of your higher self.

Gather awareness into the center of White Light and bring the consciousness of your higher self into movement with the inner planes and the soul. You are ready to unite on all systems. You are ready to focus on the development of perfect integration. You are being prepared to bring forth the vibration of the Christed Self into the physical systems.

Focus within on the vibrations of love as you move into the Mind of your own consciousness. As you enter into the place in Mind accept your connection to the guidance that oversees your own soul and spirit.

Perceive the consciousness of light, the awareness of Christ as the source of your true being. The wave of this energy is moving intently through all human egos and thus, many are confused as abruptness of change occurs in their outer life. Be still within self. Be still within the warring forces and let the armor of light and the activity of love be your calming place in the conscious mind and in the heart. Healing comes when one releases the resistance to the higher knowing and comes from that source of love within.

Perceive you are freeing your consciousness from all fear, all loss and all limitation. Accept. Do not look back! Do not walk in the past. There is inner work taking place on all planes and the intensity in the present moment is your time to perfect your state of being. The Age of Light, the Age of Aquarius is the age of movement into understanding the nature of spirit manifesting through its own creative self.

Focus on the physical and all of its elements, clearing each center. Divine love is projected passionately through the personality systems.

You are a seed, planted in the Mind of the hierarchy. You have come forth from this plane to descend into this physical to formulate your individuality as a perfect creative design. You however, have come into form and blinded by the existence of the negativity of the earth consciousness.

You have fallen into the experience in which you have perceived this third-dimensional action as a whole reality. You have acknowledged form as the only existence. You have acknowledged your full life in the conscious plane as the only existence of reality, and you have acknowledged it by participating through the power of your thought.

To acknowledge the resistance to spirit, you have accepted the wars within you and around you as the total full expression of all life. Therefore, you actively create what you have acknowledged as the only experience of life. To integrate your Higher Self you re-evaluate what you hold as the whole reality.

You recognize earth is your home. You accept the tools of the earth as an absolute part of your initiatory consciousness in the evolving self. You also acknowledge beyond this form lies the unseen experiences of light and the principalities of the unknown.

You are, in essence, participants of a total new expression of spirit. You are participating in a Cosmic Event bringing into motion a new evolving experience of the human conscious activity. You are a participant and a precursor to what will unfold in the decades of the Golden Age of Light.

Acknowledge you are experiencing in this moment the imprint and implant of the power of the Kundalini Fire energy. Accept you are connecting soul to Mind, Mind to body and body to the world of the physical. The sword of wisdom and truth is imprinted and implanted.

Experience the connection of yourself to a higher vibration as the Kundalini Fire Energy. Fully release any shadow of doubt, any negative intent and any fallen form of conscious mind, emotion or perception.

To be empowered accept and entrust the act of love as an integral part of yourself. Experience the connection of the Kundalini Fire Energy from soul to body. The act of love, a physical human experience is a binding of souls into one. It is empowering you and it is the release of energy from all levels. It is the ecstasy of body, conscious mind and soul as one. The union of the bodies, mind and the soul through the Divine Love can never be severed by thoughts.

It is the quest of your heart to experience a bond of love that completes and fulfills the body, mind and soul. Acknowledge its complete fulfillment in your life and release the fear of accepting love, of being loved, of finding love, of being love unfolding.

The power you exist in the moment is a minute power in which you will expand to beyond this third-dimensional form. When the imprint and implant of the Cosmic Christ is interrelated to you as soul, you will know power beyond any expression of this physical knowledge.

The door to this experience cannot be opened until self has been balanced through all planes. This Kundalini Fire Energy power misdirected, can explode and terminate a certain part of your commitment to growth. The difficulty of this Kundalini state of being is manifesting the power to walk a straighter path. Again, as you approach this particular experience, you have been given the knowledge to follow your innermost desire.

The vibration of the Scarlet Ray and the Kundalini Fire Energy is not to be activated within planetary network of light.

It is to be an experience of self-to-self. Experience in the moment, your total consciousness and feel the power of self-uniting all planes.

Silence

When you are cleared and awakened from this meditation, once again you will experience intense energy throughout your total physical, mental and emotional bodies. Your body has received intense vibrations beyond the normal experience of the energy of your environment. Fear not. If the body trembles, it is releasing particles of resistance.

And now, you will begin to find your thought, your awareness and your egos once again descending back into the physical. When you awaken, acknowledge yourself as complete and whole and free, and go in peace.

Congratulations!   You have completed all the planetary lightwork.

It is a crossroad in your path.

From the channel …

The cd brings a very special process. The following information is channeled for this session.

"The listening to this particular experience is by choice. It is not recommended that you work with this each and every day. It is recommended that this becomes a part of your experience throughout your life. There will be times when you are drawn to connect with this once again. It is recommended that it become just a part of a sacred session of integration. Your higher self, your inner being leads you to when this is important for you.

There may be reactions in your system even before you begin this work, this session. There may be moments when the body seems extremely challenged. There may be symptoms arise that almost break down your sense of balance. It is the preparation, beloved ones, it is the beginning of the experience, do not fear it just receive it."

Just completing the compiling this level of *A Course in Light* is a powerful accomplishment. Through the editing and channeling of the meditations for the cd's I have noticed so many personal changes After my own completion of this work, it is so wonderful to feel released from all the conditions of the past.   There is a definite shift in every part of the body, mind and soul.

From this point on, your meditations and experience change. You are now ready to enter into the angelic levels of the light.

The angelic levels are related to the origin of your creation and the frequencies are different than the chakra centers of the Soul Body of Light.

The Angelic Levels are very different and I can't wait for you to be an *Angel on Assignment*.

Antoinette Moltzan

To order Series 5
of
A Course in Light
Angels on Assignment

Go to website:

www.courseinlight.net to order

or email: courseinlight@earthlink.net

9978560R0017

Made in the USA
Charleston, SC
28 October 2011